Making Practical Sense of Career Management :

A Comprehensive Guide for Modern Career Coaching

Mina Brown and Paula Asinof

First Edition: March 2017

ISBN-13: 978-1544662480
ISBN-10: 1544662483

Dedication

To coaching students, career consultants and practitioners, and our hundreds
of clients who inspired the development of this workbook because of the challenge
of providing distinctive service in a rapidly changing and complex world of
career management and job search.

Table of Contents

APPENDIX

Introduction

Welcome to the New Age of Career Management Coaching!

In today's coaching environment, perhaps more than 70% of professional coaching involves career coaching in various aspects. Often coaching engagements, especially in the business or executive arena, include helping clients figure out what to do with their careers, how to advance in a company, or how to conduct a job search.

This workbook delivers essential competencies, tools, and methods necessary to expertly support clients in the world of modern career management coaching. By learning the powerful tools and models that come from decades of research about performance and communication excellence along with the expert skills identified as core competencies by the industry, veteran and new coaches will gain a level of career coaching mastery that reflects today's "best practices."

Chapter 1: The Career Environment and Coaching In It Today

Environment of Careers

The U.S. labor force is shrinking . . . rapidly.

Back in 2007, 66 percent of Americans had a job or were actively seeking work. By 2013, that number shrank to 63.2 percent — its lowest level since 1978.

For workers ages 16 and up. Shaded areas indicate recession. (Data from Bureau of Labor Statistics)

Source: The Washington Post, September 6, 2013

The main factors contributing to this situation are:

- Baby boomers retiring at an increasing rate.

- A recession economy keeping workers in school or at home with young families and out of the workforce. In addition, the share of mothers who do not work outside the home is increasing, after decades of decline. This shift appears to be *driven by a mix of demographic, economic and societal factors, including rising immigration as well as a downturn in women's labor force participation, and is set against a backdrop of continued public ambivalence about the impact of working mothers on young children. Source: Pew Research Center*

- More workers going on disability insurance. We believe this is because there is less stigma in being disabled and in accepting help. There is also more awareness, sensitivity, and case law related to certain disabilities, like chronic fatigue syndrome, stress-related disability, and recovery from illness.

Jobs are shifting geographically . . . radically.

Despite the growing number of sophisticated tools and technologies that support working remotely, current job trends contradict the assumption that more jobs are appearing in more places. In reality, jobs are clustering into fewer locations, mainly in innovation hubs, like San Francisco and Boston. The point is that no matter what the job is, whether self-employed or working for a company, where a person lives really matters. It affects lifestyles, finances, values, health, and especially careers.

In his book, *The New Geography of Jobs*, Enrico Moretti explains:

> *An unprecedented redistribution of American jobs, population, and wealth is under way, and it is likely to accelerate in the years to come. . . . [He reveals] this "new geography of jobs" is benefiting centers of innovation like San Francisco, Austin, Durham, and Boston. Moretti's ground breaking research shows that you don't have to be a scientist or an engineer to thrive in one of these brain hubs.*
>
> *Among the beneficiaries are the workers who support the "idea creators"—the carpenters, hair stylists, personal trainers, lawyers, doctors, and teachers. In fact, Moretti has shown that for every new innovation job in a city, five additional non-innovation jobs are created, and those workers earn higher salaries than their counterparts in other urban areas. . . . . A new map is being drawn, and it's not about red versus blue or rich versus poor.*
>
> *The rise of American brain hubs is causing huge geographic disparities in education, income, life expectancy, family stability, and political engagement. Dealing with this split—encouraging growth in the hubs while arresting the decline elsewhere—will be the challenge of the century.*
>
> *The New Geography of Jobs, Enrico Moretti*

Other trends are affecting how people get jobs and at what rate.

A variety of other trends are having a significant effect, both positive and negative, on career management, job search, and income levels. Career coaches are expected to stay current on the career marketplace and employment trends. Some of the highlights below have been adapted from a *Forbes* article by Dan Schawbel.

> *The highest level trends are the skills gap, workers dropping out of the corporate system, the use of automation and outsourcing and the pressure for companies to get leaner. All of these factors have created a system where everyone is always under pressure to stay relevant, choose degrees that turn into jobs and constantly reinvent themselves. While there are a lot of obstacles to the 2015 workplace, there are also a lot of major opportunities with millions of boomers retiring and more remote working.*

Healthcare and technology are   growth industries .

The growth in healthcare and technology jobs leads the way. According to *U.S. News and World Report* in 2017, out of the "100 Best Jobs", 8 of the top 10 are in the healthcare field and the remaining are in business (statistician) and technology (computer systems analyst).

Hiring systems and processes are broken, overly complex, and poorly managed.

While computer-based hiring systems are supposed to make the screening and selection process more efficient and effective, in actual practice, they have become unwieldy and unreliable. It has become more important than ever to have a broad strategy for networking and overall job search.

More Millennials are taking leadership roles.

In 2015, Millennials became the largest percentage of the workforce for the first time. As older leaders retire and as companies come to grips with the loss middle managers during the economic downturn, Millennials are benefiting from increased opportunities to accelerate their careers in management. In a study by CareerBuilder, 38% of the workforce is already managed by Millennials. A common problem these new managers are having is that they are unprepared for leadership positions. They were never trained on how to be good managers and are being pushed into these roles out of necessity.

The skills gap continues to widen, although this common perception is being challenged.

Often employers say that they can't find qualified candidates for open positions, and they attribute that to the skills gap. However, employers are also seeking candidates with specific skills certifications. There is evidence to suggest that the skills gap is actually an experience gap as companies prefer to hire candidates with very specific work experience, and our educational system is not well-aligned with these kinds of business needs. Furthermore, employers are also frustrated with the difficulty in finding candidates who hold the workplace values they desire (e.g. dependability, punctuality, follow-though, work ethic, professional presentation, communication skills). Consequently, internship and apprenticeship programs have risen to help mitigate this issue.

The continuous job search picks up.

Employees today are more mobile than ever. Younger employees actually expect to move to different jobs with different companies in 3-5 years. Long-term employment with one company isn't seen as desirable even if it were possible. More couples are managing two professional careers, so that if one spouse has a job opportunity that requires a geographic move, the other has to be flexible to change jobs relatively quickly. Finally, when the economy is strong, more employees are likely to explore their career options. As a result, employees are undergoing a continuous job search and have become more adept at finding new jobs. Networking sites and other technology resources help to make this possible.

Mobile hiring and the mobile job search explode.

There is an increasing emphasis on mobile recruiting—job seekers use smartphones to search for job openings as well as to apply for jobs. Career coaches must stay current on the development of new recruiting technologies, channels, and methodologies.

Social media posts are being used to attract and retain talent.

Companies have finally embraced social media as a source for attracting talent. Recruiters are becoming far savvier about building talent communities through social media. For employees or potential candidates, this is an engagement process, not a single transaction.

Millennial women are closing the earnings gaps.

While there continues to be a wage gap between the sexes, the good news is that Millennial women are finally closing it. According to a study by Pew Research, Millennial women earn 93 cents for every dollar earned by men.

More people are stepping out of traditional career paths.

Either from choice or necessity, more employees are becoming freelancers, contractors, or business owners—now referred to as "the gig economy." Companies are looking to hire more temp workers and consultants because they provide more flexibility and are more cost effective. Also, freelancing is seen as a more legitimate and obtainable career path. *"Employment in the gig economy is growing far faster than traditional payroll employment, according to a 2016 study from the Metropolitan Policy Program at the Brookings Institution."* Technology is making it easier to find freelance work, and since technology is always improving, these numbers are growing year over year. The lure of owning a business and having the imagined freedom, time flexibility, and financial returns is attracting people of all ages.

Corporate Environment

Today's world of corporate talent and career management is dramatically different from what it was even 10 years ago. At the heart of this transformation is a continuing shift toward individual responsibility for careers balanced with corporate support. And companies are increasingly seeking help from sophisticated technology for talent acquisition, employee development, and career management.

The company as the "caretaker of careers" is dead.

In the evolution of building strong contributors to organizations, approaches that blend individual responsibility for careers with company needs and interests become paramount. Using the Individual Development Plan (IDP) as a foundation, organizations with a commitment to leadership development and team performance can create a process that is meaningful to employees, encourages support from management, and actually drives implementation. In addition, a sound development model can include facilitated group sessions that align well with professionals that do training, train-the-trainer, program roll-outs, or career coaching.

Individual replacement planning for long-term talent in specific jobs is dead.

In the past, companies often used a one-to-one succession plan. The leading companies of today, however, have developed the use of talent pools. These talent pools create internal "bench strength" that align with anticipated company, industry, and market drivers. This strategy better acknowledges the uncertainty of future organizational needs and the availability of specific human resources.

Lifetime career management is the emerging paradigm for developing talent as reflected not only in the business and academic literature but also increasingly in the practices of leading organizations. When executed well, these practices blend employee responsibility with organizational support.

Sophisticated technology is rapidly expanding for corporate talent acquisition and management.

Corporations are making massive investments in talent management systems that integrate with core HR systems and with their much larger Enterprise Resource Planning (ERP) ecosystems. Talent management modules included in these systems cover all phases of the talent lifecycle: planning, recruiting, performance, learning, career development, succession planning, compensation, talent reviews, and measuring and reporting.

A key module, the Applicant Tracking System (ATS), is a software application that enables the electronic handling of recruitment needs. In many cases they filter applications and resumes automatically based on given criteria such as keywords, skills, former employers, years of experience, and schools attended. Recent system enhancements include use of artificial intelligence tools and natural language processing to facilitate intelligent guided semantic search capabilities offered through cloud-based platforms. Companies now score and sort resumes with better alignment to the job requirements and descriptions. And all of this can happen before a hiring manager even reads a candidate's name. Accordingly, many candidates are adopting resume optimization techniques similar to those used in search engine optimization when creating and formatting their resumes.

These systems have become so complex that some recruiters work around them to find candidates. One alternative is for recruiters to create social network talent communities. This cultivates relationships with potential candidates or the people they know. Often these talent communities are the first stops for sourcing candidates. Employee referrals recorded on job applications have become more valuable as recruiters will often look for these first. In some cases companies are simply using ATSs for compliance and risk mitigation.

The Coaching Industry

The International Coach Federation (ICF), the best known independent certifying body today, was founded in 1995 and has over 20,000 members around the world. According to a report published by the ICF in partnership with PricewaterhouseCoopers, it is estimated that there are 47,500 professional coaches worldwide. However, because the field is not tightly regulated, it is difficult to know the exact number of coaches. Today's coaches come from a myriad of backgrounds and professions including human resources, business, law, teaching, psychology, counseling, and more.

Coaching is not regulated by the states (yet), but the marketplace is increasingly demanding coaches who are professionally trained, credentialed, and demonstrate a continuing commitment to professional development.

What is Coaching?

Typically, coaches are amiable, compassionate people who desire to help others. However, coaching is not about being "nice". Coaching is a process whereby the coach challenges the coachee to muster all their skills, knowledge, instinct, and resources to overcome limitations and achieve whatever it is they want. From another perspective, the coach is in charge of the ***process*** and the coachee is in charge of the ***content***. If coaches get sucked into the content ("the story"), they lose their ability to best serve the clients' real issues and desire for growth.

Coaching is flourishing throughout organizations of all kinds across the globe because it's really good at getting results. In other words, efficacy is a coach's greatest strength. A good description is offered in the book *Best Practice in Performance Coaching*:

> *Coaches open up a space inside the coachee in which there is room to look around, see what is no longer required, what might be rearranged and where there are gaps that could be filled. A good coach will support, listen, and direct the coachee's focus forward to the future. The result for coachees is that they make decisions with conviction and are more likely to stick to plans which they have come up with themselves.*

As a refresher, the entire text of the ICF Coaching Competencies is included in the Appendix. Further information and reference material are available on the ICF website at www.coachfederation.org.

The Seven Principles of Coaching

Review the model that follows, then complete the exercise below.

Source: Best Practice in Performance Coaching, page 10

Exercise: Challenge Questions

1. What do you think each principle means in the context of coaching?

_____

_____

_____

_____

_____

_____

_____

_____

_____

_____

_____

2. For each principle, describe would it be like or what would happen in a coaching environment if this principle were missing?

_____

_____

_____

_____

_____

_____

_____

_____

Coaching is NOT Therapy

How is coaching distinct from other similar professions? Professional coaching is a service that focuses on an individual's life as it relates to goal setting, outcome creation, and personal change management. In an effort to understand what a coach is, it can be helpful to distinguish coaching from other professions that provide personal or organizational support.

- **Therapy:** Coaching can be distinguished from therapy in a number of ways. First, coaching is a profession that supports personal and professional growth and development based on individual-initiated change in pursuit of specific actionable outcomes. These outcomes are linked to personal or professional success. Coaching is forward moving and future focused. Therapy, on the other hand, deals with healing pain, dysfunction, and conflict within an individual or a relationship between two or more individuals. The focus is often on resolving difficulties arising from the past which hamper an individual's emotional functioning in the present, improving overall psychological functioning, and dealing with present life and work circumstances in more emotionally healthy ways. Therapy outcomes often include improved emotional states. While positive feelings may be a natural outcome of coaching, the primary focus is on creating actionable strategies for achieving specific goals in one's work or personal life. The emphasis in a coaching relationship is on action, accountability, and follow through.

- **Consulting:** Consultants may be retained by individuals or organizations for the purpose of accessing specialized expertise. While consulting approaches vary widely, there is often an assumption that the consultant diagnoses problems and prescribes and sometimes implements solutions. In general, the assumption with coaching is that individuals or teams are capable of generating their own solutions, with the coach supplying supportive, discovery-based approaches and frameworks.

- **Mentoring:** Mentoring, which can be thought of as guiding from one's own experience or sharing of experience in a specific area of industry or career development, is sometimes confused with coaching. Although some coaches provide mentoring in addition to their coaching services, (i.e. coaches mentoring new coaches), coaches do not behave as and are not (typically) mentors to those they coach.

- **Training:** Training programs are based on the acquisition of certain learning objectives as set out by the trainer or instructor. Though objectives are clarified in the coaching process, they are set by the individual or team being coached with guidance provided by the coach. Training also assumes a linear learning path which coincides with an established curriculum. Coaching is less linear without a set curriculum plan.

Where Does Career Coaching Fit?

Understanding the differences between coaching, consulting, and training is especially important for Career Coaching. The truth is that good Career Coaches use all these. The issue is "what role is most appropriate and most effective for the situation with your client?" Consider this continuum, moving from content and decision-making (left side) to process management and facilitation (right side).

Directing | Diagnosing (Therapy) | Consulting | Teaching | Mentoring | Coaching

Since Career Coaching should *not* involve directing or diagnosing in any fashion, we do not need to explore those roles in this discussion.

For our starting place, the consultant, teacher, or trainer is the content expert. They have specific content knowledge and expertise relevant to an issue while the client has the process or environmental knowledge. In this case, the content expertise governs the outcome, assuming the client accepts the consultant's recommendation or training.

At the other end of our continuum is the coach as facilitator and master of the process. At the coaching end of the continuum, the roles are reversed: the client has the content knowledge. The coach's role is to enable the client to discover insights, identify challenges and goals, and create solutions that come from his or her experiences, needs, values, and beliefs. As such, the process expertise governs the outcome.

Coaches offer questions, provide a framework of inquiry, challenge assumptions, and probe for deeper meanings and alignment. Instead of bringing knowledge, coaches bring process: professional skills that enable clients to build on what they know in order to derive a suitable solution.

Expert consultants on the other hand bring their deep expertise, strategy, structures, and methodologies to the client engagement. They are the expert problem solver. They assess the situation and provide opinions and recommendations for implementing the fix.

So where does Career Coaching fall in the continuum? It has both coaching and expert qualities. Career Coaches often move in and out of all the roles on the continuum to meet their clients' needs. They are consultants, trainers, mentors, and coaches. In Career Coaching, there is a collaboration-zone along the continuum that sees Career Coaches and clients forming a partnership of knowledge and process. A coach is there to reflect back the client's knowledge, probe for clarity, and guide the process. If, in the moment, the client has a specific problem and the consultant has an "expert" solution, it would be counterproductive to be tethered by roles and titles and not provide important and relevant expertise. Usually Career Coaches operate in the middle of the continuum, in the collaborative zone where the partnership is most productive.

In fact, we think it is more appropriate and definitely more accurate to use the term "Consultative Career Coach" or "Career Coaching Consultant." Even the simple Career Consultant or Career Adviser would have more integrity. But the market probably doesn't care. And sometimes Career Consultant or Adviser can be misinterpreted as someone who helps you find a job (e.g. outplacement). Finally, unless you are a licensed therapist or counselor, you should not use Career Counselor.

Ethics and Professionalism

The first ICF competency is "Meeting Ethical Guidelines and Professional Standards."

> **Meeting Ethical Guidelines and Professional Standards** - Understanding of coaching ethics and standards and ability to apply them appropriately in all coaching situations
>
> a. Understands and exhibits in own behaviors the ICF Standards of Conduct,
> b. Understands and follows all ICF Ethical Guidelines,
> c. Clearly communicates the distinctions between coaching, consulting, psychotherapy and other support professions,
> d. Refers client to another support professional as needed, knowing when this is needed and the available resources.

Ethics guidelines and professional standards are important issues in coaching. Since coaches are privy to sensitive business and personal information, it is essential that **strict confidentiality be maintained at all times** and that coaches act in an ethical and professional manner.

Take time now to read the **ICF Code of Ethics** in the Resources section. Career Coaching presents several unique ethics issues in practice.

Confidentiality

Coaching content is confidential—period. Clients may talk about their coaching with whomever and whenever they choose. The coach may not. **Challenge Question:** How might this be a challenge for the Career Coach?

_____

_____

_____

_____

Boundaries

There is a common market misperception that a Career Coach will help a client find a job. You will occasionally get inquiries from potential new clients who have this expectation. While there are many ways you will be able to help, you are not a client representative. **Challenge Question:** What ways will you ensure understanding and create clarity with your clients about the outcomes they can expect?

_____

_____

_____

_____

Agreements

As we will discuss later, you should probably conduct a "prequalification or exploratory" discussion with potential clients. In this process, you will be able to pinpoint what your clients' needs are and what services you can offer that are appropriate. While verbal agreements are technically valid under the law in some jurisdictions, they are extremely difficult to enforce and might often require some form of documentation anyway. More importantly, having a clear understanding with your client about the scope and deliverables of your service along with fees and payment terms is critical for good business and customer relationships. The bottom line is that coaching agreements should be done in writing. In fact, having a clear client agreement is the second ICF competency. **Challenge Question:** What do you think could interfere with a Career Coach getting a written agreement in place?

_____

_____

_____

_____

Sharing Connections

A Career Coach might be tapped for making introductions to their contacts for their Clients. We teach them about networking, networking, networking, right? So why would we be surprised if they discover that we know someone they would like to be connected to and then ask for us to make the introduction? **Challenge Question:** What issues does this present to the Career Coach and how do you handle them?

_____

_____

_____

_____

Impact of Career Coaching on Current Employer

Whether you are an Internal or External Coach paid by the sponsor company, there may be times when your employee-client decides it's in his or her best interests to leave the company. However, this might not appear to be what is in the best interests of the sponsor company. **Challenge Question:** What is your duty or obligation in a situation like this—to the employee and to the company?

_____

_____

_____

_____

Chapter 2: Intro to NLP and Communication Excellence

A fundamental competency in coaching is the ability to communicate effectively and manage the relationship with the client. The ICF competencies (detailed in the Appendix) specifically address "Co-Creating the Relationship" and "Communicating Effectively." Among the most powerful tools and methodologies in coaching come from the study of neuroscience and human performance. Neuro-Linguistic Programming is one of the most robust bodies of knowledge for application to successful coaching.

What is Neuro-Linguistic Programming (NLP)

NLP stands for Neuro-Linguistic Programming, a name that encompasses the three most influential components involved in producing human experience: neurology, language and programming. The neurological system regulates how our bodies function, language determines how we interface and communicate with other people and our programming determines the kinds of models of the world we create. Neuro-Linguistic Programming describes the fundamental dynamics between mind (neuro) and language (linguistic) and how their interplay affects our body and behavior (programming).

NLP is a pragmatic school of thought that addresses the many levels involved in being human. NLP is a multi-dimensional process that involves the development of behavioral competence and flexibility, but also involves strategic thinking and an understanding of the mental and cognitive processes behind behavior. NLP provides tools and skills for the development of states of individual excellence, but it also establishes a system of empowering beliefs and presuppositions about what human beings are, what communication is and what the process of change is all about. At another level, NLP is about self-discovery, exploring identity and mission. It also provides a framework for understanding and relating to the 'spiritual' or metaphysical part of human experience that goes beyond us as individuals and reaches out to our family, community and global systems. NLP is not only about competence and excellence, it is about wisdom and vision.

> "NLP could be the most important synthesis of knowledge about human communication since the explosion of humanistic psychology in the Sixties."
> Source: Science Digest

Since its beginnings NLP has branched into many disciplines worldwide. It has been incorporated not only into therapy, but also business, education, sports, work with animals, and more, including coaching. There are hundreds of books and articles describing processes and techniques derived from NLP.

NLP is a Framework for Success

NLP is a unique model of how people learn, motivate themselves, and change their behavior to achieve excellence in any endeavor. It offers the opportunity and skills to achieve any professional or personal goal requiring either change in style, behavior or interpersonal skills. With a good NLP foundation, a coach has a new level of understanding and capabilities to deliver on the "best practices" of coaching.

NLP is an Attitude

Those who learn NLP develop an attitude of curiosity about people and an approach to interaction with others that utilizes each experience as an opportunity to learn. These new ways of thinking and reacting provide the conscious choice and flexibility of behavior to dramatically enhance motivation, performance, decision-making, creativity, learning and emotional comfort.

NLP is a Technology

NLP offers specific, proven techniques and procedures for achieving predictable results in a wide range of contexts including business, education, personal growth, training and therapy.

NLP is a Methodology

NLP reveals the structure of behavior, communication and change. This structure can be modeled, learned and taught, thus NLP can be used to reproduce any form of high-quality performance in human behavior.

Six Important Coaching Related NLP Presuppositions

NLP has a fundamental set of assumptions that are necessary for understanding and applying all the principles. These assumptions are called "Presuppositions". Since NLP has been around for over 30 years, and there have been many important contributors to this body of knowledge, these Presuppositions have evolved. Depending on whose work you are reading, you will find slightly different versions of these Presuppositions. Below are **6 Presuppositions** that are particularly relevant for coaching.

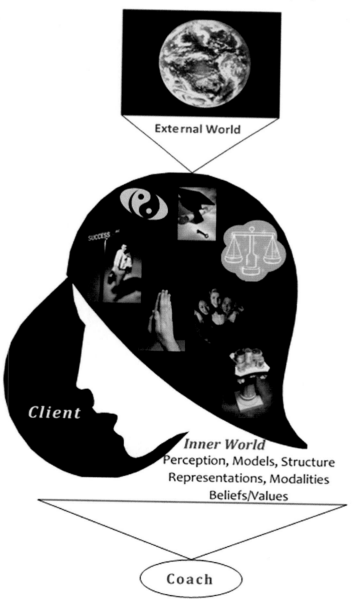

1. **The map is not the territory.** People respond to their map of reality, not to reality itself. NLP is the science of changing these maps (not reality).

2. **Requisite variety.** The element in a system with the most flexibility will be the controlling element.

3. **People always make the best choice available to them at the time** (though often there are better ones).

4. **Choice is better than no choice.** Not having a choice is a "default" response. Choices give you the freedom to select the one that will be most useful in a particular circumstance.

5. **There is no such thing as failure, only feedback.** Every response can be utilized.

6. **We are all responsible for creating our own experience.** Even when challenging events happen that we cannot control, we are responsible for our responses to these events. Typically, however, we have much more control than we think we have. Another way of stating this presupposition is that "We consistently create our own environment" through our beliefs, filters, capabilities and behaviors.

Exercise: Understanding the Presuppositions for Coaching

Answer the following questions one Presupposition at a time:

- **Put this Presupposition into your own words. What do you think it means?**
- **How does this Presupposition help you coach?**

1. **The map is not the territory.**

_____

_____

_____

_____

_____

_____

_____

2. **Requisite variety.** The element in a system with the most flexibility will be the controlling element.

_____

_____

_____

_____

_____

_____

_____

_____

_____

3. **People always make the best choice available to them at the time.**

_____

_____

_____

_____

_____

_____

_____

4. Choice is better than no choice.

_____
_____
_____
_____
_____
_____
_____
_____

5. There is no such thing as failure, only feedback.

_____
_____
_____
_____
_____
_____
_____
_____

6. We are all responsible for creating our own experience.

_____
_____
_____
_____
_____
_____
_____
_____

Chapter 3: Overview of Intentional Career Management

In applying coaching to career management, how careers develop is important to understand. Many people have allowed their careers to be conducted by "happenstance". A series of jobs—and thus their careers—happen to them, rather than the other way around. A former boss takes a new job and calls to recruit the former employee. A job is eliminated or someone is fired, and they reach out to find the next, quickest job. It's a job-to-job sequencing, with little to no long-term planning.

The more satisfying and most successful careers come from having a vision of an "ideal" future and a long-term career goal and then creating a systematic plan or strategy to accomplish it, which is the essence of "Intentional Career Management."

The concept is relatively simple but rarely executed: it's about managing one's career the same way a business is managed. Vision – Strategy (5-8 year Long-term Plan) – Tactical Plan (1 year Short-term Plan) – Next Steps – "Rinse and Repeat."

Unquestionably there are plenty of variables, uncontrollable conditions, and unpredictable situations that will impact success. All businesses face such circumstances. But planning is still essential. Companies don't abandon or ignore the planning process just because there are so many variables and unknowns. The more planning that is done, the better prepared most people are to adapt. A clear and thoughtful plan provides the "rudder" to keep the process on course. It also provides invaluable guideposts for decision making over the years as random opportunities or challenges present themselves.

Intentional Career Management Model

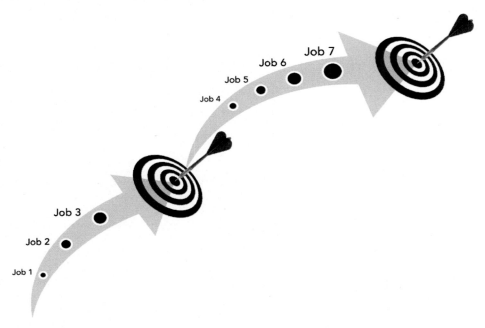

Vision

The first step is to create a clear and compelling vision of the "future state"—the ideal job the client wants one of these days. The focus needs to be at least 5-7 years into the future—far enough out that more possibilities exist. Try to keep the client in the future, not the present. This should be a "dream job" kind of description. Probe to add details—plenty of details—so that the vision comes alive in the client's mind's eye and heart. It should be exciting and naturally engenders maximum commitment.

Some suggested questions to ask a client are:

- What kind of environment do you want to be working in?
- What functional role do you want to focus on?
- What physically will you be doing? What activities will you be engaged in?
- What level of managerial responsibilities do you want?
- Where do you want to be living and working (geographic desires)?
- What industries are you attracted to?
- What kind of company do you want to work in (publicly traded/private/family-owned/government/not-for-profit and large/medium/small)?
- How much money do you want to make?
- What kind of people will you be working with?
- How much stability versus independence or freedom do you need?
- What will be different from today?
- What are you willing to give up? What are your priorities? What are the trade-offs?

Exercise: Soliciting a Career Vision from a Client

Work through a career visioning exercise. Review the questions above and add any of your own that might intensify the experience and stimulate motivation and commitment by your client. It might be helpful to imagine having this conversation with someone you know well or perhaps someone famous who's biography is familiar to you.

_____

_____

_____

_____

_____

_____

_____

_____

_____

_____

_____

Strategy

Once the vision is firmly established, the client needs a strategy for how to get from here to there. This is like a "gap analysis" for a business plan or almost any other planning activity. The coach can guide the client's thinking to determine:

- What is needed in the future? Experience, education, location, industry, other credentials, relationships . . . .
- What does the client have now—from that list?
- What are the specific pieces that the client needs to develop or acquire to accomplish the goal?
- What is the most logical sequence of activities for achieving these objectives?
- What are the priorities?
- Is there any "low-hanging fruit" that can be knocked off quickly and easily?
- What will the client start with?

From this starting position, the client can create a tactical plan.

Tactical Plan

The tactical plan is a specific game plan for achieving the next most important goal. It's not normally a one-step activity that lands a person in their forever dream job. The best way to think about the tactical plan is chunking the overall strategy into interim steps and goals. For example, if the ultimate goal is a career in a different function, perhaps the most important step is to move to a different company in the current function first but where the desired function is more central to the new company's business model. Knowing the next part of the plan brings the client to the specific next steps.

Next Steps

By narrowing the focus on an achievable next stage, the coach can help the client develop a detailed plan that can be executed. What are the specific next steps for moving forward? Are there job search skills to learn: networking, interviewing, talking about one's self, redesigning or revising marketing documents like the resume or LinkedIn profile? The client should identify which individuals to seek out who can be of assistance. Have the client consider the following overriding guideline: *Make is easy for others to help you. Be very specific in your request. Be courageous. Ask for help.*

Rinse and Repeat

Once the client achieves a major career goal, or any portion of it, the process is iterative and continuous. Each new job allows the client to confirm his/her ultimate goal or adjust as necessary. Having a well-established process in place for intentional career choices all along the way will help ensure a successful, satisfying, and rewarding career.

Chapter 4: Prospect Situation Assessment

When a potential client expresses interest in working with the coach, an important first step is the process of evaluating the situation and determining how the coach can best help. This often referred to as a "prequalification or exploratory" process, the outcome of which might be a proposal for work, referral to another professional, or a determination that there is not a good fit with this person or at this time.

Overview of Client Situation (Prequalification or Exploratory)

With any new client, the coach should be able to scope the engagement appropriately and set reasonable expectations about the process and results.

Description of the Process

The desired outcome here is to match the client with the appropriate type and level of services within their time constraints and budget parameters. It also provides the opportunity to build rapport and credibility with a prospective client in a relaxed and informative manner. The coach may have to listen to a little more of the client's back story than is absolutely necessary. The coach may also choose to provide some suggestions for their consideration, such as read a book, go to a job transition group, or encourage them to pursue additional education or certifications if appropriate.

The process for an Independent Career Coach is different in several respects from the process needed by an Internal Career Coach. Each one of the Discussion Guides are broadly scripted to help quickly qualify and assess the fit of this prospect with the coach's services or the opportunity to make referrals to other resources. As the process is refined, there may be additional questions specific to the coach's business. Also, the order of the questions may be altered as experience shows what is most effective. Finally, these are intended to guide a personal conversation with the client and are <u>not</u> to be used as a fill-in-the-blanks form to send out in advance. Clients have enough forms to fill out without getting another one from a coach. And the coach will miss out on the essential benefit of building trust, gaining credibility, and adding a personal touch to the process.

Independent Career Coach (External to an Organization)

Preparation:

Have available:

- A blank prospect information form (a sample form is included in the Appendix)
- A summary of service offerings—what's included, what's not included, prices and various other options
- A summary of affiliates for referral purposes—what they offer (probably stay away from their prices except for a reasonable range)
- A listing of free or inexpensive resources to use for directing people who are not a fit for the coach's services or prices

The coach will probably receive personal referrals, unsolicited phone calls, emails, requests for information from a website, and other sources of inquiries. To be effective in sales activities, the coach should be prepared to respond quickly. *You snooze, you lose.* If it takes too long for the coach to get back to prospects, there is a good chance they will find their services elsewhere.

Exploratory Discussion Guide - Independent

1. Confirm who you are talking to and get contact information (phone & email)
2. Ask "what kind of work do you do?" Drill down until you have a function and a level and an industry.
3. Ask what is the purpose for which they need [whatever they have indicated they need, e.g. career coaching, a resume, interviewing, career services, job search strategy] *at this time?*
4. Depending on the answer, you may need to determine how quickly they need it.
5. Depending on their level and sometimes on what you offer, you may need to determine if they have a budget in mind.
6. Sometimes you will want to ask their age and compensation.
7. You are now in a position to offer them options that match their needs. This may be a selection of services you offer, a referral to a colleague, or a combination of both.
8. You may also be able to offer some high level guidance that is relevant and useful for their situation, including where to go if you don't provide the services they are looking for, other resources for people who can't afford your fees, or sometimes advice on obvious deficits or issues presented in the discussion (e.g. lack of education, missing crucial certifications, inconsistent goals).
9. In closing the discussion, next steps might include:
   - Schedule the appointment—get a date locked in.
   - Confirm logistics—where will you be meeting.
   - Provide instructions for making payment; get the deposit over the phone if applicable.
   - Discuss advance preparation requirements.
   - Get it all in writing—send a confirmation email.
10. If applicable, send follow-up email(s) for any referrals to other colleagues

Note: The coach's responses are driven by the prospect's previous answers. It takes some time to become comfortable with the flow but practice helps. *Keep in mind the goal is to get clients, not to provide free consulting.*

Internal Career Coach (Within an Organization)

Potential "clients" might come to (or be sent to) HR for Career Management services from:
- A succession planning process
- A performance review action step (good review, bad review)
- An organizational change
- A high-potential candidate nomination
- An identified need for an Individual Development Plan

Preparation:

- If appropriate/available, pull the employee's personnel file to become familiar with his/her background.
- Gather internal materials relevant to the topic, such as training resources, forms, job postings.
- Identify relevant corporate policies.

Exploratory Discussion Guide - Internal

1. Record the name and contact information (phone & email) of the person and his/her supervisor.
2. Ask the following questions:
   * What *specifically* has caused you to be here at this time? (Don't assume you know it from their perspective.)
   * What is the intended goal from the process?
   * What is the time frame?
   * What is the budget?
   * What is your boss' expectation and level of involvement (does your boss even know you are here)?
   * What expectations do you have about confidentiality?
   * What have you done previously in regard to this goal?
   * What is your level of commitment to this effort?
3. You are now in a position to offer options that match their needs. This may be a selection of internal activities, external programs or services that fit the budget, or a combination of both.
4. Clarify each person's role and responsibilities in the process.
5. In closing the discussion, next steps might include:
   * Schedule the appointment—get a date locked in.
   * Confirm logistics—where will you be meeting.
   * Discuss advance preparation requirements.
   * Complete registration or company mandated documentation.
   * Get it all in writing—send a confirmation email.
6. Send email follow-up with boss or other key person, as appropriate.

Importance of Clarity

We cannot overstate how important it is to conduct a thorough and well-organized prequalification or exploratory process. The most important outcomes, other than checking for fit and chemistry, is to:

* Gather information about and clarify the client's issues and goals.
* Set boundaries and expectations about deliverables and fees.
* Explicitly communicate limitations on documents, time line, and ability to achieve desired results.

Keep in mind that not all engagements are "good" or viable. The career coach should be judicious about taking on any engagement where there are concerns about the expected outcomes and the coach's ability to perform. When it doesn't feel right, it probably isn't a good fit—things can end badly for everyone. It is okay (and prudent) to turn down some clients—just say no, and trust the Universe.

Exercise: Case Studies

In order to gain more confidence and develop skills in applying these questions, the following case studies present a series of hypothetical statements made by prospective client. The challenge in this exercise is to take on the role of a career coach and outline your approach or targeted questions for these individuals in order to get to the essence of the clients' needs. No need to ask every discussion question for purposes of this exercise. Just evaluate how you can get to the root issue(s) so that you can effectively direct the discussion of your services. Some of the case studies are examples of external clients and some are internal.

Here's an example. Your potential client says, **"I can't seem to get any interviews. I need a new resume."** Your approach might be to say the following.

Based on my experience, you probably could improve your resume, and we can help you with that. (This is to validate that you heard their concern or perspective.) It's possible that your resume is not the entire problem. You may not have a good job search strategy. You may not be networking adequately. What specifically are you doing in your job search activities? What percentage of your job search efforts are you spending responding to job postings on the Internet? In the eye of a future employer, how would you compare to other candidates? What other factors may be affecting your results? Are there challenges or pitfalls in your work history that may require special handling?

Case Studies:

1. I find myself at a crossroads in my career where I am not sure where to go next and how to get there in the company. What I know for certain is that my current path is not fulfilling.

   _____

   _____

   _____

   _____

   _____

2. I'm interested in speaking with someone about my CV. I had one professionally done two years ago but I have not had any success with it and I think it needs to be reviewed and possibly rewritten.

   _____

   _____

   _____

   _____

   _____

3. My boss gave me a horrible performance review. I'm hoping to bid on a job in another department, and this might block the possibility.

_____

_____

_____

_____

_____

4. I am an "all in or all out" kind of manager. I'm working too many hours to conduct a job search. So I've decided to turn in my two-week notice on Monday. I need a good resume to find a new job.

_____

_____

_____

_____

_____

5. I graduate next month and my parents say I have to have a job by the end of the summer.

_____

_____

_____

_____

_____

6. I want to relocate to a new city, but I can't move without a job. I haven't had any luck applying online. Any assistance you can provide would be appreciated.

_____

_____

_____

_____

_____

7. I am looking to work on rebranding my image. I am a surgical technician working on my nursing degree. It has been many years since I've updated my resume and quite frankly, I am not sure where to start.

_____

_____

_____

_____

_____

8. In my mid-year review, my boss shared with me that I have been included on the succession planning list for two key jobs. She told me to come talk to you.

_____

_____

_____

_____

_____

9. I am looking for a resume writer and interview/career coaching. A company I have been with for 17 years in progressive increasing roles has recently been purchased by an outside group of investors. I'm not sure of the direction and culture this company is heading and want to keep my options open. I would like to talk with somebody and understand what you offer to help me move through a possible change.

_____

_____

_____

_____

_____

10. I'm interested in getting help on deciding next steps in a career path then creating a resume so that I can find the "perfect" job for me.

_____

_____

_____

_____

_____

Chapter 5: Structured Program to Define a Career Strategy

Some clients will simply want to focus on their immediate issues or needs. For these clients the best approach might be a laser-focused session called a "Career Jump Start." This 2-hour session is a "classic" coaching session where the coach starts with the client's coaching goal and helps the client quickly create a clear and realistic outcome. Then the coach facilitates a discussion about what the client can do differently to be successful, including identifying barriers and creating action plans.

A more comprehensive and long-term focused approach can be conducted with more time to invest, such as a 4-session program with 1.5 – 2 hour sessions spread over 4 – 8 weeks. The greatest benefit to this approach is the ability to start with the long-term career goal even if it's a bit "out there." It's like starting with a clean sheet of paper or a blank white board, without getting bogged down by how to get there at the beginning. It allows the client to dream about their ideal job and situation.

The more challenging, remote, or degree of change the goal represents, the more sessions it may take. Some of the work between sessions may be for the client to gather more information, confirm his/her assumptions, test reality of marketplace, and complete other tasks that nail down the goals and test the vision for reasonableness. The ultimate objective is for the client 1) to feel inspired and motivated to achieve the goal, 2) have a clear set of action plans to get there, and 3) know exactly what the next steps need to be to move forward.

Here's a suggested approach and structure for four coaching sessions aimed at discovering the "perfect job" and creating an inspiring yet practical action plan to assist the client in getting it.

The coach guides the client through the following steps:

Session 1: Defining, as clearly and fully as possible, the future "dream job". Identifying potential unknowns, critical assumptions, and fit with personal priorities. (Usually 2 hours)

Session 2: Refining and confirming the future "dream job" and clarifying specific requirements and critical success factors. Assessing current capabilities/credentials and inventorying missing ingredients. (Usually 2 hours)

Session 3: Creating a broad plan for closing the career development gap and performing a reality check. (Usually 1.5 to 2 hours)

Session 4: Completing a detailed action plan for immediate next steps and the "perfect" NEXT job that will align with career intentions. (Usually 1.5 to 2 hours)

Normally there is research and fieldwork that occurs between each session. So, the program usually spans a month at the shortest and typically longer, 8 – 10 weeks, depending on how much work needs to be done in between sessions and also what else is going on in the client's life. If the vision and strategy is defined in less than 4 sessions, the remaining sessions can be used to focus on the client's weaker skills such as networking, talking about themselves, or interviewing.

Exercise: Case Studies

These case studies are similar to the ones in the previous exercise except this time you are given descriptions of the client rather than original statements they make when they first call in. For each situation, consider these questions and jot down what you are curious about.

- What are the possible realities of this person's employment situation?
- What options could be available to this person?
- What is the impact of their decisions right now on the rest of their career?
- What are the coaching questions you would ask?

Case Studies:

1. A recent graduate from a small college in Tennessee with an excellent academic track record in math and economics wants to move to a metropolitan area and secure a high-profile job.

_____

_____

_____

_____

2. A competent middle manager who has received excellent performance ratings has not been selected as a candidate for a director-level position. He believes his career may be stalled for some reason and wants to advance, either in this company or another one.

_____

_____

_____

_____

3. A sales and account management executive with a Fortune 100 company and a 20-year tenure believes it is time to "move on" and doesn't know exactly what that is.

_____

_____

_____

_____

4. A 50+ year old successful corporate executive has made some lateral moves in the last 8-10 years but seems to be looked over for more senior positions when they become available.

_____

_____

_____

_____

5. A multi-talented former consultant, entrepreneur, and global project manager who looks her age of 58 (or older) wants to find a "really cool job" that would utilize her breadth of experience and talents. Coworkers would undoubtedly be decades younger.

_____

_____

_____

_____

Chapter 6: The Job Search Process

Too many times job seeker starts their job search process with updating (or creating) their resume. Then they spend hours and hours searching the Internet—job boards, company websites, LinkedIn—for posted jobs and completing the required applications. This is equivalent to a "ready—fire—aim" approach. This approach is rarely effective, which can result in a career coach getting a call.

Common complaints are: "I've applied to 98 jobs on line and haven't heard back from any of them. I think I need a new resume," or "I have applied for several positions in the last 8 months, but I'm pretty sure I'm not getting past the first cut. So, I have decided I need a new resume and cover letter that shout 'hire this person'." As a career coach, the best way to address this is to suggest to the client there's a lot more to it.

There is a logical and systematic way to tackle a job search, and it doesn't start with a resume. Here are the key steps in the right sequence for a successful search.

Overview of Methodology

Job Search Flow Chart

Focus
What job do you want?

Prepare
Get your act together.

Aim
Do your research.

Network
Build relationships, have an ask.

Interview
Preparation is key.

Negotiate
Factor in total economics & title.

Start Work
Get to know the players.

It is important that the client actually does the work and owns the results, while the coach serves as a guide and accountability partner. Below is a checklist for the coach to use with clients in progressing through each of the steps:

Focus

- Figure out what you want to do and where you want to work.
- Carefully define your next job, incorporating elements for which you will be considered a good candidate.

Prepare

- Develop your unique selling proposition. (Why would an employer want to hire you? Why are you qualified for and a better candidate than other applicants?)
- Create your marketing materials (e.g. resume, bio, cover letter) to be in alignment with your desired next job.
- Update (or create) your LinkedIn profile to reflect your new resume and focus.
- Start building your LinkedIn network—aggressively add connections from your current/prior jobs, industry and community activities, social sphere, and even family. (If they are not dead, they are a networking contact, no matter how you know them.)

Aim

- Research what companies have those jobs in your desired geographic area.
- Create a Target List of companies you want to work for.
- Identify key people in those companies with whom you want to connect.

Network

- Be specific—make it easy for people to help you.
- Ask for introductions to your target list of people and companies.
- Check company websites and job boards for positions that might interest you.

Interview

- Prepare thoroughly for each interview—preparation is more than 75% of a good interview.
- Take practice interviews—your first interview should not be your ideal job if possible.
- Follow up religiously.

Negotiate

- Evaluate all economic facets of the offer.
- Counter-offer to ask for more money or other benefits (e.g. title, vacation time)
- Keep selling all the way to the end.

Start work

- Priority one—get to know all the key people around you.
- Deliver exceptional performance—ask questions if you don't know something.
- Continue to network—never stop.

Once the focus and targeted job is clear for clients, they then move to creating career documents that are tightly aligned with their goals.

Chapter 7: Stand-Out Personal Marketing

The foundation of career marketing documents is a well-articulated, tightly focused introduction. It is the short and effective answer to the ubiquitous question "Tell me about yourself." This question strikes fear into the hearts of some of the most successful people. As career coaches, helping a client craft a good answer to this question and be able to deliver it articulately is powerful. It is key not only for interactions with others such as interviews and networking but also for building the client's self-knowledge and confidence.

Just as important, the personal introduction becomes the Summary section at the beginning of the resume. It is crucial that in just a few phrases and key words, the personal introduction nails the message to the listener or reader. It also becomes part of the Summary section on the client's LinkedIn profile and drives and Executive Bio.

Why Is a Personal Introduction So Hard for People?

Here are some reasons people give for why it is difficult to introduce themselves with clarity, polish and pizzazz.

- I believe it's impolite to brag.
- I don't think I'm personally worthy.
- I don't know what to say.
- It's none of their business.
- I'm embarrassed to talk about myself.
- I'm not confident enough to put myself in the limelight.
- I feel insincere.
- It feels superficial.
- I'm afraid that people will judge me.
- The other person really doesn't want to know about me.
- I'm shy.
- It's too personal.
- No matter how much I prepare, I don't seem to be ready.
- In my culture, it is inappropriate for people to talk about themselves.

Fear or Embarrassment Comes from Several Sources

Cultural Bias

Every culture has its own view of what is considered polite. Many cultures frown on people who talk continuously about themselves and their accomplishments. While it is okay for someone else to describe other people in glowing terms, it is generally considered impolite to say the same things about themselves.

Emotional Resistance

Fear of being judged is one of the most common reasons for poor personal introductions. People tend to be far more aware of their weaknesses than of their strengths. Indeed, many people have such high expectations for themselves that they have a hard time focusing on and talking about what they do well. Learning how to "pitch yourself" is empowering. The very act of crafting a personal introduction produces a sense of accomplishment and a higher level of self-esteem.

Assumptions

People make assumptions every day. They are an important part of getting things done in the fast-paced world we live in. But if they are rushed or distracted, these assumptions will often turn out to be self-defeating. When asked to describe ourselves, for example, it is easy to assume that people aren't really interested or assume that the answer will sound superficial or insincere. Done poorly, it actually may be superficial and insincere. A good introduction must not only be factually accurate, but it must also be from the heart. The personal introduction is used in interviewing which is discussed later in the Workbook.

Career Marketing Documents

The number and kind of career documents has exploded. Each one has a specific purpose. Regardless of what document is being used, it is a piece of **personal marketing communications**. It should be designed with the target audience in mind. It must communicate relevant information and deliver key messages in a way that can be easily understood and absorbed quickly.

For a Career Coach, helping a client create these documents is far more involved than just producing a product. It involves asking the probing questions, uncovering the right focus, facilitating personal ownership, and coaching the client to success.

Clients who seek career coaching and help with their career documents fully expect the coach to have competence and expertise in this area. This program provides significant resources for the coach to leverage their specific field experience. Clients bring their expertise about their goals, their career, their job history, and their professional environment. In addition, clients often look to their Career Coach to help them decide what information to include. Ultimately, the client can use as a guide their assessment about what the next employer will care about.

This table summarizes the most common career documents today.

Types	*What it is*	*How it is used*
Resume	Marketing document that presents comprehensive career information and branding/positioning—one to three pages of succinct and targeted value-added information	Used to apply for jobs, internal and external, as well as consideration for organization boards, college applications, awards, and more
Bio	Short, one-page introductory story-telling document designed to engage a reader	Useful for networking, informational meetings, job search process, and numerous professional applications including websites, speaker introductions, and more
Curriculum Vitae (CV)	Credentialing document usually several pages long with comprehensive career information and extensive details regarding education, academic and professional achievements, publications, grants, and more	Used primarily in the academic, scientific/medical, research environments. In Europe and some other regions, the "CV" terminology is more commonly used and may be more of a hybrid of the CV and the resume.

Types	What it is	How it is used
Creative Resume	Artistic portfolio piece	Used by creative professionals to display their talents and style
Federal Government Resume	Rigidly crafted resume consisting of several pages required to comply with federal government job specifications	Only style of resume acceptable for federal government job applications
Mobile Friendly Resume	Resume specifically designed for easy reading on a smartphone or tablet	Increasingly recruiters are using mobile devices to review resumes
Business Cards	Personal calling card containing your key contact information for sharing with the public	Used to share contact information in networking, interviewing, and other non-job search activities
Executive Profile	One-page combination resume and bio which often includes a headshot, testimonials or other eye-catching information	Primarily used by senior executives and entrepreneurs to provide an engaging high-level overview of their capabilities/services
LinkedIn Profile	Comprehensive information provided in a variety of ways on a person's LinkedIn page—more is better	Used for making connections in business and job search
Cover Letter	One-page introductory letter (document) that sometimes accompanies a resume	Used to highlight key elements of alignment of the candidate and the job opportunity
Email Cover	Typical cover letter but in an email format	Used in conjunction with email attachments of resumes, cover letters, and other related documents
Thank you note	Brief follow up note, either handwritten or in an email	Used after a meaningful meeting or interview that helps to reinforce key messages and keep the process moving forward
Job Application	Legal document detailing career and personal information, typically electronic	Entry into the candidate screening process and often required by companies for compliance
Personal Website	Website on a personal domain that displays career history, portfolios (as applicable), photos, and other interesting content	Used for personal branding, marketing, and increasing visibility
References	One-page summary of key references that can be shared at the appropriate time in a job search	When requested by hiring company, provided to validate candidate's experience, qualifications, and personal characteristics
Portfolio	Compendium of work products related to various careers, such as creative, consulting, legal, or financial	Used to provide examples of work to establish the candidate's work quality and style

Included in the Appendix are sample resumes and bios.

The Resume Writing Process

If you ask 20 different people what a good resume looks like, you will probably get 20 different opinions. Everyone is an expert about resumes. Ultimately, the only opinion that really matters is from the person who has a job to fill.

Hiring managers and recruiters are "customers", and resumes should be designed to communicate in alignment with what they want to buy and in their language. It may seem strange to think of resumes as part of a basic sales process, but resumes are like marketing brochures—they are part of the candidate's marketing and sales collateral.

It is estimated that readers initially spend 6-20 seconds reviewing a resume. Therefore, the format and layout must communicate key information in a way that is easy to absorb quickly and is "on message."

What's wrong with many resumes is that writers are talking to themselves about themselves rather than talking to customers about their needs and objectives in hiring for a specific job.

There are a variety of ways to create resumes. No matter what approach is used, the candidate must supply the content. A coach or resume writer can help in structuring and prodding to capture more information, but the candidate is responsible for providing all the data, content, and context. Resume writers are not mind-readers. The best resume writers are not experts in all jobs and industries, but they do bring considerable knowledge and awareness of job markets, industries, functional areas, technical terminology, and other relevant aspects to a job search. Whichever approach is selected, it needs to be systematic and efficient. This builds the coach's credibility with the client and enables delivering a quality product at a reasonable price.

Usually it is counterproductive to try fixing someone else's resume or other documents. First, more time will be spent trying to fix existing formatting than if it is built from scratch. Second, working from someone else's ideas about what's important and how to present it can undermine the ultimate quality of the document—odds are neither the client nor the resume writer will be completely happy with the result. And finally, the client could have a misperception about the amount of time and energy it takes since there was something to "start with."

Traditional Resume Writing Approach

Traditionally, the resume writer gathers information from the client and uses it to create the first draft of a resume. The information can be provided from existing documents (e.g. previous resumes), filling out forms with key data, or in a consultative discussion—in person or by phone.

The resume writer assembles the information into a format appropriate for the circumstances and sends a draft to the client for review. After making changes, the resume is complete. This could take more than one iteration.

Most people do not like filling out 25-page forms. That's often why they come to a professional to get the resume done in the first place. They also are counting on the professional resume writer to guide them on best practices.

Coach Approach Resume Writing—Interactive Development

An alternative approach is to develop the resume real-time directly with the client, either face-to-face or by phone. In this approach, the resume writer does minimal work when the client is not present. In building the resume with the client, the document becomes the client's document not the resume writer's. Not only does the client have a document they are proud of but they also know every decision that has been made in its creation, how the document is structured, and how to work with it to adapt it based on specific opportunities. The end result is a document that evolves as it is used by the client.

While the output of this approach is designed to be a high-quality document and experience with the client, it does take a particular personality to conduct as well as the right kind of client. The resume writer must be able to work in real-time with clients and their information, not just in gathering information but also in producing the final document. The client should be willing and able to participate fully in the process. Generally, this process does not work well for people who lack good communication or language skills. This process also requires a meaningful commitment of time by the client, and thus is not a good solution or approach for everyone.

Creative Gobbledygook

The world of resume writing is ever-changing. We frequently see "interesting" resumes that include:

- colored headings, borders, or text
- fancy, non-standard fonts
- pictures, graphics, icons
- graphs
- columns
- call-out boxes
- strange and stranger formats

There is also buzz about video resumes, infographic resumes, QR codes sprinkled everywhere, and more and more gobbledygook. Yikes!

What are the readers of the resumes really looking for? Do they want to see a video resume? Do they care about colors, fonts, pictures, and other graphic elements? Is it even being "read" by a human? What happens to the format when it's opened on someone else's machine or phone (if it even can be opened)?

For some jobs, maybe yes. For most jobs, probably no. Compelling content, alignment with job requirements, easy reading, and clear messaging are what count. No amount of color, graphics, or sexy presentation can make up for lack of content, poor fit, or clutter.

One Resume for Humans and Computers?

Now, more than ever, computers are just as likely to review a resume as a human being. For several years, the resume writing industry has cultivated multi-purposed resume design. In other words, one resume can serve many needs, including automated screening.

Based on the difficulty of creating such a document, it is often more effective to create separate documents than trying to do it all with just one. Resumes are frequently processed through front-end text converters before they are loaded into searchable databases, such as applicant tracking systems.

A standard "pretty" resume can become garbled or unreadable as it passes into large database systems. Furthermore, it is likely the candidate will not know what front-end process is being used and what their resume will end up looking like. By editing the unformatted or text version of the resume, the automated search results may be improved once the resume is in the database.

The Importance of Setting Yourself Apart

Unfortunately, most people present themselves with an inward focus, an emphasis on their own objectives, their career histories, and the details of their accomplishments—their view of what is important. It makes a great biography but not a good customer-facing presentation. Newsflash! When candidates presents themselves, it's not all about them. It's only about them in the context of what the customer is interested in.

This brings us to the concept of "Positioning." In marketing, positioning means the process by which marketers try to create an image or identity in the minds of their target markets for their products, brands, or organizations. Positioning is extremely useful for describing the alignment of the candidates' talents with the needs of the organization and highlighting the value of their contributions. That is, after all, how matches will be made.

Identifying Positioning Keywords

When a job search starts, hiring managers have a few key items that are essential to their hiring decisions. This list may be conscious or unconscious ("I'll know it when I see it"). And frequently, this list is not exactly the same as position-standard skill sets. Who is this person really trying to hire? What are the skills and characteristics that make a difference to the hiring manager? A good place to start is with a short list of keywords that align, as best they can, with these requirements. If it's not a perfect match, it's okay to ignore what's missing. Carefully reading job posts or gathering other information about this position or similar positions is a rich source of ideas.

Many of the jobs clients apply for may need small modifications to their resumes to effectively sell themselves. That doesn't mean they have to create entirely different resumes for each position. For a good multi-purpose resume, a set of generic positioning key words can be created based on common themes across several jobs. Then, these key words can be manipulated according to the targeted audience. Remember, there is always a customer out there. The objective is to identify what the customer wants to buy and help them make the "right" purchasing decision.

Format for Positioning on the Resume

HEADLINE (Who You Are)
Subhead (Narrow the Field)

Positioning text – (five-line paragraph using phrases, not full sentences). Lorem ipsum sed dolor sit amet, con sectetuer adipiscing elit, sed diam nonummy nibh euismod tincidunt ut laoreet dolore magna aliquam erat volutpat. Ut wisi enim ad minim veniam, quis nostrud exerci tation ullamcorper suscipit lobortis nisl ut aliquip ex ea commodo consequat. Duis autem vel eum iriure dolor in hendrerit in vulputate velit esse molestie dolore eu feugiat nulla facilisis at vero eros et accumsan et ipsum dolor sit amet, consectetuer adipiscing elit, sed.

Keyword (Functional Skills)
Technologies, Methodologies or Other Appropriate Sub-line, for example lower level skills – or delete this line
Keyword (Personal Characteristics)

Positioning Paragraph Worksheet

When gathering information for the paragraph in the positioning section, using a worksheet like the one below to capture notes is helpful. Ask the client the following questions, and record notes in their own words. Allow them to talk freely, like stream of consciousness. Use whatever colloquial language they present, and specifically encourage them to describe things fully, without "self-editing." There is no judgment or right or wrong in compiling this data.

1. **Love:** What do you love about what you do? What is your mission, your passion? What about your work gets you up in the morning and keeps you motivated?

2. **Good:** What makes you good at what you do? What innate abilities, unique talents, or special gifts do you have that others don't? How specifically do you think about things that contributes to your success?

3. **Like:** Why do people like to work with you? These people include peers, bosses, employees, internal staff, customers/clients, vendors, regulators, politicians, and others.

4. **Say:** What do people say about you? What would a reference say? What positive things have been documented in performance appraisals and letters of recommendation? How does the press characterize you? In a nutshell, why should I bring you into my organization?

Here is a sample positioning worksheets. These are notes that try to capture actually what the person says in their words. Colloquial language is fine. Stream of conscientiousness is fine.

Love:	growing and developing people, advising and counseling on better ways to deliver solutions, taking on extremely hard challenges and finding unique solutions, love challenging, learning, growing, challenging the status quo, ideas that have always been in place, love seeing people who I've worked with evolve and become better people and leaders, love winning, love work that I'm passionate about, love making a difference in people's lives with the Company's products we deliver, giving back to the community
Good:	great listener, creative problem solver, pull seemingly disparate pieces of information together to create unique solutions, passion and conviction, truly put team before myself, thinks about things as biz problem 1st so fully appreciate what we are trying to deliver, very balanced approach to looking at the world, data, feelings, motivations, emotions and can pull it all together to drive innovative solutions
Like:	smart, thoughtful, look for team wins vs individual wins, not afraid to give unpopular advice, care about people I work with and committed to their growth, deep experience and understand mistakes made and learn from those, seen a lot and can translate that in an effective way, funny, passion – people like to work around people who are passionate and successful and optimistic
Say:	trusted advisor, great influencer, great communicator, deep experience in human capital, knows what he's doing, creative problem solver, direct but fair, great motivator of teams, great followership, others want to work for and with him, deep understanding of organizations and people and why they do what they do, cares deeply about his team and the organization. He will accurately access the changes and find solutions to fix them.

From these notes, the Career Coach can draft the positioning paragraph. It is a skill that takes time and practice to acquire. The client will have neither the time nor the interest to invest in becoming adept at creating it. If they choose to do it, it may have to be re-written, which produces frustration and disappointment.

The positioning paragraph should be a well-crafted work of art that reflects the candidate's unique value and talents. It is normally 4-5 lines written in phrases rather than complete sentences. This paragraph is central to the candidate's ability to present themselves articulately and to engage their audiences. As much as possible, help the client build pictures or metaphors in their descriptions.

The top of a resume is created by combining the headline, subheading, and key word lines with the positioning paragraph. Here is an example using the sample worksheet above.

HR EXECUTIVE – BUSINESS UNIT PARTNER
Growing Medium to Large Businesses

Charismatic leader who leaves a mark on an organization and its people not only with innovative approaches but also by making a difference in employees' lives, the company's products and the community it serves. Trusted advisor with a gift for pulling together disparate pieces of information to create unique solutions. Based on deep human capital experience, challenges existing business practices and finds methods that drive productivity, help people grow and strengthen the culture. Good listener with inclusive and optimistic style.

Transformational Growth – Strategic & Tactical Implementation – Human Capital Solutions
Performance Management – Coaching – Talent Acquisition – HR Program Delivery – Community Involvement
Passionate Leader – Forward Thinker – Analytical Problem Solver – Collaborative – Influencer

---

Exercise: Co-create Positioning Statement with Client

We strongly suggest you find a volunteer to help you with this exercise. While it can be done on your own by imagining yourself as the client, it's far more meaningful to engage in the creative dialogue with someone else.

Questions	Notes
Love	
Good	
Like	
Say	

Draft of the Positioning Statement:

_____

_____

_____

_____

_____

_____

_____

_____

Chapter 8: Coaching Opportunities in Resumes and Bios

Developing a resume as part of a coaching relationship provides numerous opportunities to facilitate clients' thinking about their careers, their approaches to advancement inside or outside their current roles, and their job searches in general.

Reframing: Shifting Key Perspectives

Reframing is based on the idea that meaning depends on a person's point of view. In working with clients on their resumes, two key perspectives are useful in setting the stage for not only a good resume but also a deeper understanding of themselves, their career choices, and their job searches.

1. *There is a customer on the "other side" of every resume. The resume reader is making a purchase decision, and the client wants to help the reader make the "right one".* This changes a resume from being a compendium of past experiences, skills, and accomplishments to a document that aligns the client as well as possible with what the recruiter/hiring manager (the customer) wants to buy.

   The client whose resume is a laundry list of the past is saying to the reader, "Here are all the great things I have done (accomplishments) or can do (skills), so what job do you have for me?" Instead, the client should be saying "I am exactly the person you need to hire because my knowledge, skills, and abilities – as proven in previous jobs – are well-aligned with your (stated) needs."

   Powerful Question: *"Do you think it matters to your next employer?"* Ask this question when a client asks, "Should I include this?" or "Is this important"? If it does matter, include it. If it doesn't, don't. How will they know? The content of job postings is a good place to start. Are employers requesting that experience or skill from prospective candidates?

2. *The more senior the client, the more a resume needs to shift from a focus on competency to a focus on contribution in order to stand out and differentiate him/herself from the pack.* At senior levels, some competencies are assumed (e.g. the CFO can do a budget). Other competencies that not everyone has should be made explicit in the "context of" a contribution (e.g. a CFO was instrumental in the company's successful IPO, therefore, that CFO has competency in doing IPO's). At more junior levels or in roles that are not accomplishment driven, the competencies should show up in the "context of" job responsibilities emphasizing the important characteristics such as "how many," "how much," "how long," "how complex," or "over what geographies."

   Powerful Question: For executives and other leaders, *"What was the essential value that you delivered to the company in this job – or across several jobs?"* *"Is there a theme that runs through your career?"* You many need to drill down a few times to actually get the client thinking this way. Once this has been established, it can help clients focus on the kinds of career and job choices where they bring value and are likely to be successful.

   For others, *"What are the attributes of your job that show the depth and breadth of your knowledge and responsibilities?"* *"What is the magnitude of the role which the employer is trusting you to handle?"*

   For many clients, answers to these powerful questions are life-changing.

Coaching Opportunities – Section by Section

This table highlights some of the standard coachable areas and the coaching opportunities provided during the resume development process.

Resume Section	Coachable Areas	Powerful Questions
Contact Information	Availability to travel (50% or more) and/or relocate (globally)	What are you willing to do – really? To what extent does this open up or constrain your career opportunities? Are you (and your family) OK with that?
	Unique education or credentials in-process, high level security clearances, availability for shift/rotational schedules, citizenship	What is relevant to the employer? How does it help to highlight your value? How does it dispel potential misconceptions?
Positioning	The entire positioning section	"Tell me about yourself…." Four key questions for creating the positioning text: <ul><li>What do you love about what you do?</li><li>What makes you good at what you do?</li><li>Why do people like to work with you?</li><li>What do people say about you?</li></ul> The process of developing the heading, subhead and key word lines provides an experiential opportunity for a client to learn how to read and utilize a job posting. This is useful not only for resumes and bios but also essential for cover letter creation and interviewing preparation.
Career History	Structuring the career history	What is your career story? Is there a theme?
	Presenting accomplishments and competencies	What was the "end of the story?" How was your success measured? What accomplishments and competencies best reflect your level of responsibility?
	Headlines (optional, usually for senior levels)	What is the overall accomplishment or contribution you made in this job or at this company?
Credentials	Education, certifications and other credentials	Do you have credentials you need now or in the future? If not, which ones are most important? How will you get them? In what time frame? Do certain credentials that you have help you or hurt you – and how can this best be presented?
	Professional, civic, and community involvement	If there hasn't been much…. What are the possible downsides to not being connected into your industry or community in a meaningful way? How would you determine the best opportunities to enhance your professional and civic involvement? Under what circumstances would you include or leave off items that focus on race, religion or political preferences?
Addendum	Projects, consulting engagements, patents, publications, speaking events, media coverage	In what circumstances and in how much more detail beyond the main resume content is it important to communicate about your skills and contributions?

The Professional Bio

Good professional bios are hard to find. Bad ones are everywhere. Bios are found on websites, in marketing brochures, in sales presentations, in public profiles, and in promotional press releases—and sometimes are used for job searches. Bios are often requested by professional and philanthropic organizations considering an individual for membership or leadership roles.

Given the plethora of personal information easily available to the global community, often in the form of a bio, it is essential that business professionals attend to managing the presentation and content of this information. For those who have shied away from a public presence, it is more important than ever to establish themselves visibly. For a career to be vibrant and successful, especially in today's "gig economy," people need to be easily found and professionally presented. And a bio gives the reader their first impression of the person. A pioneering coach in the field of professional image has prophetically said "although people should be judged by their innate worth, it is often a first impression that determines whether someone will stick around long enough to let them reveal it."

A professional bios is an important tool for enhancing visibility in numerous ways. More than ever, strong positive visibility is a key component of successful lifetime career management. As career professionals, wise and competent counsel on the use of professional bios is no longer just a "nice to have" skill, but rather it is an essential competency for working with employees on an upward career trajectory.

Characteristics of Effective Bios

Most bios are dull and boring, providing little insight into the person behind the words. Bios often say "held this job, did this, held that job, did that, went to school there, grew up somewhere, married the high school sweetheart, and has 1.8 children." Change the names and locations and those bios could be about anyone. While they can be impressive in the display of credentials, essentially a mini-resume, they are not likely to engage the reader with the person.

One reason for the overwhelmingly blandness is that bios are frequently written by third parties who do not necessarily understand the individual's story or the targeted audience. These bios are simply comprised of data that has been dropped into a more or less predetermined format. In addition, many are too long with too much information. With the rise of LinkedIn, even recruiters are now turning there first, and interest in this type of bio for recruiting purposes has radically diminished.

While a "mini-resume" bio may be useful in certain circumstances, it is not enough to serve as a professional marketing tool. The best bios tell a story that entices the reader to want to get to know the person and understand his or her unique talents and value. It is a "personal press release" designed to wow the reader.

Whether used for business purposes, for advancing visibility through professional or community activities, or for job search, professionals these days must reach beyond being a commodity in an overcrowded market of similarly accomplished peers. Professionals must visibly position themselves and be recognized as thought leaders in focused areas to stand apart from the competition. In addition, the concept of "personal branding," which was taken mainstream by Tom Peters in 1997, has spawned an entire industry. The notion is now so pervasive that it took its place in the "Dummies" series of books in 2012. A well done bio is a key document for articulating a personal brand.

Bios and Professional Presence

The development of a personal-branding-focused bio often moves it from a piece of marketing communications to a vehicle that helps strengthen "executive presence". As described in the BusinessWeek article "She's Gotta Have 'It'," the "It" is presence, and the lack of "It" can prevent even the most qualified people, especially women, from achieving promotions for which they are otherwise strong contenders. As BusinessWeek describes it, "presence refers to… making a polished entrance… taking hold of a room, forging quick personal connections… inspiring that I'll-follow-you-anywhere-loyalty…conveying an aura of warmth and authenticity…." Notably, the article points out that self-confidence and self-promotion are critical.

A well-written bio frames a personal brand that is presented with conviction and panache. And, furthermore, the process of developing one with the individual fully engaged strengthens his or her ability to deliver it in person with style and confidence. Career coaches can be instrumental in assisting their clients in developing and internalizing their professional personas.

David D'Alessandro, the former Chairman and CEO of John Hancock Financial Services, makes the point explicitly: "Everyone in organizational life is constantly being watched and evaluated by bosses, clients, vendors, peers, and subordinates. Every day, with every bit of human interaction you engage in, some member of this crowd forms an opinion about you."

So whether it is the bio itself, the process of creating it, the influence on how the individual presents him or herself in person, or all of these, there is no doubt that this document properly designed, developed, and used addresses essential aspects of career management.

Collecting Feedback on Your Documents

When the client has a final draft of the career marketing documents, it is important to "test" them. Using the questions below, invite the client to share the documents with other people and collect their feedback. Encourage the client to consider all feedback and remember that just because one person has a particular opinion, that does not necessarily make it true. The client gets to decide whether to make a change or not.

How "Good" is Your Positioning, Resume, and Bio?

√	Question	What the Question Means
	Is it clear?	Does the reader immediately get a picture of the person being described?
	Is it me?	Do you recognize me, the person you know?
	Is it engaging?	Does it portray me with distinguishing and valuable capabilities and qualities?
	Does it have impact?	Does it showcase my talents?
	Does it capture the essence of my story?	Is it a "lead paragraph" flowing easily into the detail?
	Is it powerful?	Does it communicate my level of authority, responsibility, and accomplishments?

Job Search Execution: Do the Research

To properly aim a job search, it is helpful for clients to have specific companies and people identified in targeted geographies and industries. Getting information about public companies is relatively easy. Annual reports are always available and provide a huge amount of information about targeted companies. Company websites can add considerable information, especially the "News" pages. It is also important to be aware of current events impacting a targeted company.

Gathering information about privately owned companies, associations, or not-for-profit organizations can be more challenging. Knowing where to go for more obscure information is helpful in this research. In addition, there are several websites and resources for "specialty markets" such as international opportunities or retirees.

Here is a list of resources to aid in the research and cultivate a tight aim for a candidate's job search.

Tools for Targeting

- LinkedIn
- Google
- Wikipedia
- Dun & Bradstreet
- Fortune/Forbes (America's big private companies)
- Inc. Top 100 companies
- Goinglobal.com
- Hoovers
- Industry directories: AM Best, Chain Store Guide, Hospitals, and more
- IvyExec.com: Rankings (top consulting firms)
- Lexis/Nexis (lawyers)
- Local business journals' *Book of Lists*
- Local Chambers of Commerce
- Directory of Associations
- OneSource.com (subscription only, primarily used for business prospecting)
- RetiredBrains.com
- Yahoo
- Yahoo Finance (upcoming IPOs)
- Yelp
- ZoomInfo.com

Chapter 9: Networking: The Raw Power of Who You Know

Six Degrees of Separation

The early concept of social networks was popularized by Hungarian author Frigyes Karinthy in 1929. He is considered the originator of the notion of "six degrees of separation."

Later, Harvard Social Scientist, Stanley Milgram took up the "small world problem" and conducted research to quantify the number of degrees of separation in actual social networks. His 1967 study, published by Psychology Today, generated enormous publicity for the experiments, which are well known today. Milgram's study results showed that people in the United States seemed to be connected by approximately three friendship links, on average, without speculating on global linkages. He never actually used the term "six degrees of separation."

The notion of six degrees of separation or small world theory has become accepted and even influential in popular culture. It became a play in 1990 then later a movie in 1993 with Stockard Channing and Donald Sutherland. It was Will Smith's first major role. A lot of people also know about the Six Degrees of Kevin Bacon game based on this theory. More recently, in 2003, Columbia University and Carnegie Mellon created the Small World Research Project. Their research found that on average, people can reach their targets in five to seven steps.

In a world of 6.6 billion people, it does seem hard to believe. The theory of six degrees of separation contends that, because we are all linked by chains of acquaintances, you are just six introductions away from any other person on the planet. In August 2008 researchers at Microsoft confirmed the theory (almost). They studied 30 billion electronic messages among 180 million people in various countries, and determined that any two strangers are, on average, distanced by precisely 6.6 degrees of separation.

More recently, research by Milan University and Facebook, published in November 2011, suggests that the average number of connections between two people anywhere in the world is just 4.74 (just 4.37 in the United States).

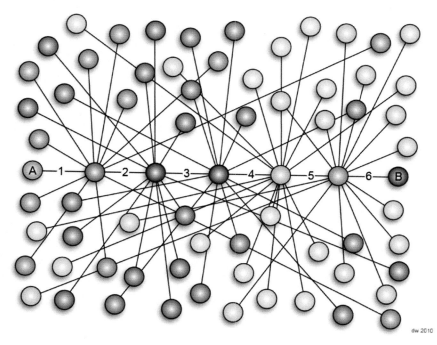

dw 2010

So why is networking so important and powerful in the job search process? Imagine that a person has 100 connections and each of those connections have 100 connections. Then how many connections does that person have at the third level?

Me (x)	My friend (L1)	Their friend (L2)	Their friend (L3)	Total	Formula for Total
100	x 100	x 100	x 100	= 100 million	
50	x 50	x 50	x 50	= 6.25 million	x^4
250	x 250	x 250	x 250	= 3.9 billion	

Reciprocity

It's hard to believe, but... networking is as valuable for the person being connected with as it is for the person connecting. In today's connected world, professional and personal connections are a key part of a "career balance sheet." The more favors someone does for others (like making introductions), the more successful that person will be in requesting help in the future.

There is networking and then there is NETWORKING. First, a candidate should organize and collect an inventory of connections before they launch into asking for help. The investment of time at this starting point will produce real benefits in the form of efficiency and focus when clients begin their search in earnest. Thus, there are two stages of networking for job search: 1) populate the contact database and 2) activate it to put it to work.

1. **Populate:** From the people who you know, add as many as possible to your contact list. LinkedIn is probably THE most important networking tool, but it's not the only way to network. It's just the easiest. A few years ago, the average number of connections on LinkedIn was 250. It's definitely increased since then. The largest grouping of users has 500-1000 connections. So no matter what number of connections a person starts with, it can be higher with a little time and attention.

2. **Activate:** When ready, but not before, start to leverage connections for specific actions. With already identified target jobs and target companies (Focus and Aim), take action. By using LinkedIn and other resources, ask connections to make introductions to these targets – not find you a job. Focus on connecting to the right people in the right places. Also, when making a request (or ask), be very specific and reasonable, creating a higher probability that the connection will be willing and able to assist and will follow through. Make it easy for other people to help you.

Exercise: Review of Networking Essentials

In this brief exercise, we invite you to think about your clients and how you can coach them more effectively in the art of interviewing. Briefly answer these questions to reinforce your understanding of networking and have a quick reference for working with your clients.

Question 1: What barriers exist to "networking" - why don't people network at all, more, or better?

_____

_____

_____

_____

_____

Question 2: What types of conversation are most effective when networking?

_____

_____

_____

_____

_____

Question 3: What are some ways to get started or get better?

_____

_____

_____

_____

_____

Question 4: Once established, how can someone make sure that they continue the relationship without feeling like they have used someone or taken advantage of the relationship?

_____

_____

_____

_____

_____

Networking Strategy Worksheet

In order to get the most value from networking efforts, it is helpful if the client is prepared for the calls or meetings and has a specific outcome in mind. It is also critical that they follow up after the encounter. Lack of follow-up is just unprofessional and makes the efforts somewhat pointless.

Here's a simple worksheet that clients can use to focus their efforts and document commitments made to each contact.

Name	Goal	Activities, Notes	Follow Up

Chapter 10: Interviewing

The 4 "P"s of Interviewing

The four essential principles to a successful interview are *Preparation, Presence, Practice, and Persistence.* Consider what ultimately produces a successful job search. Who will get the job?

- The person with the best **resume?**
- The person with the best **company contacts?**
- The most **experienced** person?
- The person who **interviews** best?

Of course if people don't have good experience or can't get in front of the right people, then they won't get the job. But even if they do all those things right, the interview is the critical step in the process to secure the job.

Preparation: Key to a Successful Interview

Essentially 75% of success in an interview happens before the candidate picks up the phone or drives in the parking lot. It comes from being well prepared. Solid preparation also contributes to the candidate's ability to demonstrate confidence, poise, and personality in the interview. Excellent preparation enables a candidate to make a good first impression, and that's something that sticks.

Preparation includes doing the research. Potential candidates need to find out everything they can about the company and the job. They need to check out both published as well as informal sources. Some of the things they are *expected* to know are:

- Company reputation and major strengths
- Major needs, challenges, risks
- Competitors, competitive position, market share
- Major products and services; operating divisions
- Primary customers and markets served
- Geographic locations
- Significant current issues
- Internal cultural norms or unique characteristics (formal or informal atmosphere)
- Major needs, challenges, or risks the company faces

Anything that is published on the company's website is fair game. In particular, the most recent company events are usually available in published press releases which can be found in the news or press sections of their websites. Here are some ideas about where to go to get more information:

- Internet Search Engines: Google, Yahoo, Bing
- Company published material—annual reports, company website, brochures
- Public relations department
- Industry publications (accessible in many libraries)
- S&P Register of Corporation Directors and Executives
- Hoovers, D&B, and similar directories
- Wall Street or other analyst reports (for publicly traded companies)
- Local Business Journals or Chambers of Commerce

Informal sources

- Employees—current and former
- Friends and family
- Competitors, Suppliers, Customers
- Recruiters
- Company receptionists

Know How to Introduce Yourself

The most common first "question" in an interview is "tell me about yourself." To be prepared for any interview, including screening calls, job seekers must have a clear and compelling way to describe who they are and why they are a competitive candidate for the job.

Real Life Interview Questions: What Are They Really Asking?

In interviews in particular, there are many interview questions that a really asking the same thing. It is useful to help the client "hear" the variations. Here are some examples.

- *Tell me about your background.* = Tell me about yourself.
- *Why should we hire you?* = Tell me about yourself.
- *Summarize your experience.* = Tell me about yourself.
- *Give me the highlights of your career.* = Tell me about yourself.
- *Why don't you walk me through your job history?* = Tell me about yourself.
- *What makes you a good candidate for this job?* = Tell me about yourself.
- *What expertise do you bring to the team?* = Tell me about yourself.

Just the Facts

The best introductions are simple, crisp, and spot on. A good approach to crafting an introduction and being comfortable saying it is to focus on the facts—just the facts. Believe or not, it is not personal—it's factual. A coach can help clients get comfortable with being able to talk about themselves in a neutral, non-emotional way.

The key questions that should be answered in an introduction are:
- Who are you?
- What do you know that is special compared to your competition?
- What do you do? What is it like to work with you? What makes you a star?

Reframing the Approach

There are some additional concepts that will help candidates get over their reluctance to talking about themselves.

- Relax and stay "in the conversation"- don't give a speech. Use colloquial language. Adapt the introduction to the specific situation regarding the agenda, the message, and time available.

- Be specific, don't just talk in generalities or "business speak". Instead, drill down to the specific attributes that set the client apart.

- Sometimes the use of third party attribution, using someone else's words and ascribing them to the speaker, eliminates the perception of bragging.

Areas for Preparation

Here are some topics where a coach can help a client with interview preparation.

Identifying Assets

- Study the resume.
- Inventory positive attributes.
- For the top 5, construct supporting statements.
  - Strong statements, bold, active.
  - Enough substance to be compelling, but not too long.

Achilles Heel

- Be prepared to handle the one or two things that are the weakest part of the resume or experience.
- Handle it with candor but create a statement that mitigates any adverse effect.

Interview Q&A

- Crisp and concise, answers should be no longer than 2 minutes.
- The ideal "talking" balance.
- Dialogue not monologue.
- Okay to pause to think first.

Preparing Questions in Advance

- NOT the time for due diligence.
- NOT about the candidate's concerns.
- NOT the time to ask about money.
- IS about showing how the candidate thinks, approaches the job, contributes.
- IS about demonstrating careful preparation and forward thinking.

And here are some key considerations for clients to keep in mind:

The "Dating Game"

- Make them fall IN LOVE.
- Convince them they have found the BEST candidate.
- Never say "No"—it's about staying in the game—especially in the early screening.
- A job can always be turned down, but if the offer is never made, it cannot be turned down or negotiated.

Interview DON'Ts

- NEVER speak badly about a former company or boss
- NEVER lie: Spin—YES, Lie—NO
- NEVER show up late
- NEVER leave home without extra resumes and business cards

Practice, Practice, Practice

- Practice with a friend or coach
- Create and maintain an "Interview Journal"
- Take some "practice" interviews, if possible
- Try not to have the first interview be the most important one

Follow Up After the Interview

- Send thank-you notes, emails are fine
- Complete an Interview Self-Assessment
- Break through the silence
- Go into recovery mode
- Bounce back from rejection

Not All Interviews Are the Same

These days, it is common for the interviewing process to go through many stages. The candidate may be put through several levels of interviews plus a variety of other steps before a final decision is made and an offer extended. It is important for candidates to understand what these stages are and the corresponding objectives.

Step	Objective
First Contact, usually a screening call [a]	General fit, interest, paperwork
Screen/Assessment Center [a]	Invest time
Comprehensive – one or more sessions [a]	Serious consideration, including hiring manager
Panel Interview	Definitely serious consideration
Peer Team	Input to decision maker, hiring manager
Boss's Peers/Customers	Input to decision maker, hiring manager
Reference Check [a, b]	Validation (agrees with your data, refutes your data, provides new information)
Boss's Boss	Usually veto, often finalist only
Degree/Background Check/Drug Test [b]	Verification
Credit Report [b]	Fiduciary *(depends on position responsibilities)*
Psychological testing [b]	Personal characteristics & fit
Informal Social *(senior level only)*	Chemistry
Board of Directors *(senior level only)*	Affirmation/courtesy, finalist(s) only, except CEO where the Board is the "hiring manager"

a) Recruiter may be involved.   b) May be conducted by an external resource.

Take Phone Interviews Seriously

This is another opportunity for the coach to serve as a guide to a client who is in the interview process. Below are the things clients who are being interviewed need to incorporate into their job searches and interview strategies and keep front of mind during the interview process.

Phone Interviews: Types

There are three basic types of phone interviews:
- First contact
  - Minimum info about you – 5-10 minutes
  - May segue into phone screen
  - Fit to general parameters, gauge interest, get paperwork
- Phone screen
  - Has paperwork
  - May be 1st or 2nd contact – 15 minutes – 1 hour
  - Decide whether to invest in you
- Phone interview
  - In depth. Treat the same as a face-to-face in terms of content and objectives

Phone Interviews: First Contact

- Take the call. Listen.
  - Market information
  - Be helpful. Build relationship
- Who are you talking to?
  - Get name and company
  - Recruiting firm, company recruiter, or hiring executive
- Don't worry how they got your name
  - If they wanted you to know, they would have told you—so you would take the call
  - Database, research, anonymous referral
  - Unlikely your boss gave it out or that you have been compromised
  - Everyone, hopefully, gets calls from recruiters. It's a good thing!
- Interested?
  - Get spec.
  - Define next steps.
- Not interested?
  - Get spec and pass on or make referral

Phone Interviews: Screen In or Out

- Be prepared
  - They have your paperwork—you have a spec
  - You researched the company
  - You have prepared to talk about yourself
  - You have prepared Q's about the job and the company (to start making your own decisions about interest)
- How long is the appointment
  - Usually 30 minutes to 1 hour
  - Pace the time
- Good place to talk
  - Quiet, uninterrupted, no distractions
- Your objective: Stay in the game
  - This is a "screen" – say "no" later unless something is clearly a show stopper and not worth wasting anyone's time
  - Communicate key messages
  - Create alignment with the job requirements
  - Find out next steps in the process

Phone Interviews: Are For Real

- Treat like a real interview
- Plus: No first impressions based on appearance
- Verbal communication is key
  - Can't read body language
  - Body language influences verbal
  - Presence still counts
  - Smile, sit up straight, feel successful – voice will communicate this
- Time may feel longer/shorter

The Do's and Don'ts of Video Interviewing

"You never get a second chance to make a first impression." Though many disagree about the origins of this quote, its truth is unanimously upheld. And when it comes to job interviews, first impressions are strategic moments. From writing an engaging cover letter accompanied by a stellar resume to conducting oneself professionally when meeting a prospective employer, it is imperative to consistently present oneself in a polished manner.

With modern communications technology changing how business is done, video interviewing is becoming one of the most prevalent employment trends. Instead of having pools of candidates come to an office for an interview, increasingly employers choose to interview remotely using video applications. It's important to take a video interview as seriously as an in-person one.

Do dress the part.

Though the interviewer will only see the top half of your body, resist the temptation to only dress the part from the waist up. Research the company's culture through their website, Facebook page and other social media outlets, and find out what the general dress code is. Then dress as if you were going to an in-person interview. There are two reasons for this: first, it will help you feel more professional, and second, in the event you need to stand up during the interview, your outfit is pulled together perfectly and you maintain your professional appearance.

Don't use technology as an excuse.

Granted, if you're not familiar with Skype or similar programs, online interviewing can be intimidating. So like any other challenge you encounter, prepare properly. Ensure your Internet connection is high-speed, and acquaint yourself ahead of time with the program. Make sure to turn off all alerts from Skype, email, cell phone texting, and other programs to minimize interruptions when speaking. And if you still don't feel confident about the technology, tell your interviewer it's your first Skype interview. Most people will react with understanding and patience if there is a technological glitch.

Do minimize background distractions.

No matter whether you live with your partner, parents, roommates or pets, make sure that nothing can disturb or distract you or your interviewer. Start with looking at the backdrop to your on-screen image: what is visible behind you? Avoid cluttered shelves or rooms; instead, find a neutral wall to frame you. In addition, make sure everybody in your environment knows not to disturb you. If you are home and have children, ask a neighbor to sit with them for an hour or so. If you have pets, make sure they won't disturb you during the interview. And don't forget to turn off your phones!

Don't forget to prepare your lighting.

One common beginner's mistake is to sit in front of a window in order to show a pleasant view. But remember, backlighting will render your features almost invisible to your interviewer. You'll only appear as a dark silhouette on the interviewer's screen. The best lighting is a soft light source approximately six feet behind your monitor and facing you. It enables good visibility without creating too much or too little light.

Do practice.

Even if you're accustomed to talking to friends and family on Skype, give an interview situation a couple of test runs with a friend. This is especially important for those who aren't used to the technology. Dress professionally and position the screen slightly further away than normal so your interviewer can see your entire upper body, including your hands. This allows the interviewer to read your body language, which is extremely important for good rapport. Ask your friend whether your voice is too loud or too soft, whether the background is neutral enough, and if there are any visible or audible distractions. Practice as many times as necessary until you feel comfortable with the technology, the setting, and your presentation.

Don't forget to make eye contact and smile.

One of the most difficult aspects of Skype interviewing is remembering how to make eye contact, something you'd naturally do during an in-person interview. Instead of looking at the screen, look into the camera. That will give interviewers the impression you're looking directly at them. And smile! It's important to maintain an engaged and pleasant facial expression throughout, so forget that you're talking to a computer screen and pretend that your interviewer is actually physically in the room with you.

Don't be intimidated.

Learn to embrace and master new interview trends.

Group or Panel Interview

Increasingly candidates are finding that group or panel interviews are part of the selection process. Group interviews are on the rise because of companies' desire to reduce turnover and minimize selection cost. Also, teamwork is more important than ever before. When several people are doing the interviewing, the risk of making a bad hire is reduced, and the interviewers are implicitly held to a higher standard of interviewing skill.

In an About.com post on December 10, 2016, Karen Schweitzer, their Business School Expert, offers a good description of these two basic types of group interviews:

> In a ***candidate group interview***, *you will most likely be put in a room with other job applicants. In many cases, these applicants will be applying for the same position that you are applying for. During a candidate group interview, you will definitely be asked to listen to information about the company and the position, and you may be asked to answer questions or participate in group exercises.*

> In a ***panel group interview***, *which is much more common than a candidate group interview, you will most likely be interviewed individually by a panel of two or more people. This type of group interview is almost always a question and answer session, but you might also be asked to participate in some type of exercise or test that simulates your potential work environment.*

Here are some tips coaches can use to help their clients prepare for either a group or panel interview:
- Use good basic interview behaviors: appearance, personal presentation, solid preparation, including questions to ask, clear communication, enthusiasm, and expressed level of interest.

- Bring enough resumes for all interviewers just in case the company did not provide them.
- Remain calm, poised, confident, and professional when faced with a group/panel interview.
- Greet interviewers individually, making note of each person's name and title to address them personally during the interview.
- If possible, collect their business cards in order to send each interviewer a personal thank you note.
- Maintain good eye contact. Address answers first to the questioner and then include other interview panelists.
- If you are being interviewed with other candidates, lead rather than follow.

Structured Interview

In a perfect world, there is a perfect structure to an interview. That never happens. In real life, there are more bad, unprepared, and unskilled interviewers than good ones. The typical flow of an interview can be anything and often is all over the map. By understanding an effective interview structure, candidates can figure out where they are in the process and know how to direct their questions.

When a coach is guiding a client in practice interviewing, understanding this structure helps the client recognize the context of the interview questions.

1. The First 5 Minutes
- The basis for chemistry match
- Basic capabilities
- High level qualification

2. Alignment with Spec
- Resume and position match
- Candidate's capabilities and contribution to company
- Domain knowledge

3. Conducting Business
- Type of environment the candidate is most comfortable in
- How the candidate gets things done by management/leadership style
- Type of people the candidate likes to work with

4. Communication and Perspective
- How people view the candidate
- How the candidate views themselves, others, organizations

5. Career and Life Management
- Career goals
- Career management skills
- Ability to travel, work different shifts and other constraints

6. Tough, Unexpected Questions
- Flexibility, quick thinking, and ability to answer succinctly

Behavioral Interviewing

The term "behavioral interview" is often used, but a candidate may not know what it means. No matter what it's called, there is a high probability that a candidate will experience this type of interview question and approach. Behavioral interviews are popular today. They are used at some point in nearly every interviewing process, even if the interviewer is not particularly skilled at the method.

Predicting the Future from the Past

A behavioral interview is designed to examine a candidate's past behaviors. It's based on the assumption that past behavior is the best predictor of future performance.

Recognizing the Behavioral Interview

In behavioral interviews, candidates will be asked to describe a time when they did something that exemplified a particular characteristic, quality, or competency that the interviewer is interested in. Most behavioral interview questions start with, "Tell me about a time when. . ." or "Give me an example of a situation when. . . ."

An interviewer may stop after the candidate answers. However, a skilled interviewer will use the answer as a jumping off point to explore the candidate's actions and rationale more fully. It becomes a dance. Since the interviewer doesn't have the answer in advance, a truly good interviewer will be able to move from the first question to the next and the next, spontaneously drilling down into the candidate's experience based on the information provided. The flow of the questions will be focused on determining if the candidate has the competencies—knowledge, skills, and abilities—needed to do the job well. The process is not just a random exploration of the candidate's past.

For example, "Tell me about a time when you had to make a critical decision in your boss' absence." Depending on the answer, the next question might be, "How could you have handled that situation differently?" or "How would you handle the same situation differently in the future?" Or, it might be "How did your boss evaluate your decision?" or "What kinds of outside influences affected the outcome of your actions?"

Keep in mind, it is not a matter of right or wrong answers. Also, some interviewers can take the process to the extreme. For example, one candidate reported that his interviewers had each been assigned a specific set of behavioral interview questions that they were required to rigidly ask. The interviewers robotically asked the questions assigned and made no attempt to build rapport. They did not engage in any exploration, conversation, or dialogue. While it made for an unpleasant experience, the candidate was well-prepared and just took it in stride.

This type of interviewing is a dance in which the interviewer starts things off but then follows the candidate's lead. Understanding how behavioral interviews work and having thoughtfully developed scenarios to draw on, the candidate can relax and go with the flow.

Keys to Powerful and Effective Interview Scenarios

Good interview preparation includes 5-8 scenarios. With just a few well thought-out and carefully crafted stories, the candidate can answer just about any behavioral interview question the interview can come up with.

Candidates should select several situations in which they were particularly proud of their performance and results. These situations may include an award, public acknowledgment, or a promotion. These "stories" can come right from resume accomplishments, or they might come from performance reviews or personal recommendations.

A few (2-3) scenarios need to be "negative" ones—experiences where the project did not go as planned, the decision was a poor one, or the result was disappointing. Describing how a negative outcome was handled can show the hiring manager a lot about character, sense of responsibility, courage, and problem solving ability. Candor and transparency could make all the difference between getting the offer and finishing in second place.

Formula for Powerful Scenarios

Complete the first three parts for every interview scenario. Then also complete parts four and five for negative scenarios.

Part 1. Problem or issue description. Briefly share the background of the situation or issue. What was the problem? Why was it an issue? What was your role or responsibility in the circumstances? Be concise and keep the details to the minimum necessary to set up the back story.

Part 2. What you did. Describe what actions you took and how you came to those decisions. Emphasize the decision making process. Indicate how you overcame obstacles or barriers. Even if the situation was a team endeavor, the focus is on your actions and your contributions.

Part 3. Outcome or results. Summarize the positive (or negative) outcome from your efforts or decisions. Include quantifiable data if possible.

* * * * *

If this scenario is a "negative" one, then the next two parts must be included.

Part 4. What you did to fix it. If the project was a bust or you had to reverse a decision you made, then indicate what steps you took to make it right and get back on track—with your customers, your employees, your boss, whoever was impacted by the outcome. Describe how you took responsibility and how you delivered a new and improved outcome.

Part 5. What you learned from the experience. We all make mistakes—no one is perfect. But you shouldn't have to learn the same lesson over and over. In an interview, you want to assure the hiring manager that you have learned an important lesson from the situation that you won't have to learn again. To cap off the happy ending, you should summarize a new process or tool that you adopted to ensure your success in similar situations in the future.

No matter what scenario you share, conclude it with a "happy ending."

Exercise: Practice Interview

The best way to coach a candidate on their interviewing skills is to just do it. In this exercise, recruit a partner to work with you. Conduct a practice interview session as the interviewer first, then ask your partner to interview you so that you can experience being the interviewee. After each session, make notes about the experience and anything that will help you coach your own client on their interviewing. You might practice using the following Post-Interview Self-Assessment form which can help candidates hone their interviewing skills over time.

Post-Interview Self-Assessment

Company	
Position	
Interviewer, Title	
Contact Info	
Venue	__In-person __Telephone
Date and Length of Interview	
Strengths	
Areas for Improvement	
Ability to Engage the Interviewer	__High __ Medium __Low Comments:
Specific Recommendations	
Questions/Answers to Remember	
Follow Up Action Items	__Thank You __Documents? __Status? __Other?

Resources for Interview Coaching

Included in the Appendix is a comprehensive Interview Preparation Worksheet. This is a handy tool that can be adapted to help candidates think through the information they need to prepare in advance. Trying to think about these things extemporaneously, on the spot, is foolish and can even be seen as unprofessional to the recruiter. Some of the items, of course, may not apply to everyone.

Talking about Money (or Not)

How questions about compensation should be handled depend upon where the candidate is in the interview process. Many candidates mistake compensation questions in the early stages as a negotiation. Rather, early questions are ones of scope – does this candidate fit within our compensation range? For example, if a position is targeted for $80 – 90,000, a candidate who is currently making $30,000 is most likely too inexperienced. On the other hand, for a candidate who requires $150,000, this position usually will not be suitable. In the early stages, the screener is trying to determine if the candidate is in the ballpark for fit and if the company should invest more time.

Unless something is totally out of whack, though, candidates are better off avoiding the conversation about money if at all possible. In theory, if the job requirements, scope and other factors are a good fit, then the compensation package will most likely reflect a fair market value that is reasonable. If candidates do give a salary number, there are two possible outcomes: 1) if they give a number that is too low, they may have left money on the table when they get an offer, or 2) if the number is too high, they may be eliminated from consideration altogether.

The question of money is almost certainly going to come up in the early screening stages of the process. There is a certain amount of finesse that can be deployed at this point, and the coach can help the candidate craft the best answer to the question.

Not All Money Questions Are the Same

Recruiters are trained to vet candidates for compensation fit. The best recruiters know what to ask. Less experienced ones, not so much. Consider each of these questions and how a candidate should answer.

- What are you looking for?
- How much money do you want to make?
- What salary are you aiming for?
- What did you make in your last job?
- What's your current salary?

In the first three questions, the interviewer is asking for a hypothetical or desired income. If the question is posed in this fashion, candidates are best served by offering an acceptable range or avoiding the question completely. If the interviewer persists, candidates can simply ask the interviewer what the range is for the position. Assuming it is even close, candidates can give a positive response and move forward in the process. Another answer could be a broadly qualifying statement like, "Based on my understanding of the job requirements, responsibilities and scope of the job, I'm sure the market range will be acceptable." Remember, compensation is negotiable, but candidates don't get the opportunity to negotiate if they ultimately don't get an offer. And they can't get an offer if they don't get an interview.

In the last two questions, the interviewer is actually asking for facts, data, not speculation. Dodging that question makes the candidate seem squirrely. It's best to give a straight forward answer. Things to consider would include 1) giving an average of the last two or three years if there has been a downward fluctuation for some reason (e.g. variable compensation factors, bonuses, commissions), 2) sharing a total cash compensation number that includes bonuses and any other unusually generous benefits like lucrative 401(k) matches, and 3) briefly explaining why the latest salary does not reflect the targeted salary, either way too high or way too low. This might be in a situation where a candidate was making a very large salary in a prior position but is looking for a career change that they know will produce significantly lower pay. Another situation might be where a candidate stepped into a lowing paying job for a period of time for some reason and now is aiming for a more competitive and appropriate

Offer Negotiation

Congratulations! A candidate has mastered the job interviews, left all the competitors in the dust, and entered the final phase of the job search: compensation negotiation.

What is likely to happen? Way too often candidates don't actually negotiate their salary or the host of other compensation elements. Typically, the company clarified salary expectations early in the process, so that now they just make the offer. Amazingly, real negotiations do not happen. Candidates don't even consider making a counteroffer. And they don't realize or think about all the components that may be negotiable.

Do not underestimate the long-term impact of even small differences in compensation. Getting the next salary right will influence the next one and the one after that and so on. Getting a raise or a title change after being hired is much more difficult than negotiating those things before being hired.

In working with the client, the coach can encourage the candidate to bravely ask for more money. When asking for more money, it is important for the candidate to keep "selling" their excitement and fit for the job. There is a strong possibility that if their counteroffer is within reason, the company will go for it. At least they might come back with something a little better. It's important for the candidate to remember that they are the last "man" standing. They are the chosen one—the company has painstakingly determined they are the BEST. So leverage has now shifted to the candidate's favor.

While salary is the most obvious factor in the negotiation, there are many other things that can be negotiated. What are the ones the most common ones?

_____

_____

_____

_____

_____

_____

_____

_____

According to an executive search and outplacement firm, here are 33 things other than starting salary you can negotiate.

1. Job title as of start date
2. Job title after trial period or after 12 months
3. Promotion after trial period
4. Waiver of trial period
5. A signing bonus/arrival fee
6. Company assets
7. Executive education: define how many days per year and the budget
8. Guaranteed bonus in year 1
9. Waiver of the competition clause if you are in sales
10. Car/car allowance/payment of car leasing
11. Public transportation pass
12. Upgrade for flights
13. Frequent flyer miles to keep (not always the case)
14. Size and location of office
15. Home office arrangements
16. Flexibility in working hours
17. Date of next salary negotiation
18. Increase in salary after trial period
19. Housing (total or partial)
20. Relocation allowances
21. Admissions to associations or business clubs
22. School loan reimbursement
23. Annual medical check-up
24. Discounts on company products and services
25. Better insurances: health, dental, vision, disability, life, accidental death
26. More paid time off (PTO): sick day handling, personal days, paid holidays, vacation (how many, when and how)
27. Time off for charity/community work
28. Sports and recreation: fitness club, golf or other membership fees
29. Equipment: notebook, mobile phone
30. Personal usage of assigned assets
31. Special commissions on deals brought in and ownership of customer lists contributed
32. Timing when commissions, bonuses, or other incentive compensation vests
33. And finally: "OK, what did I forget? What else could be negotiable?"

John F. Kennedy said "Let us never negotiate out of fear but let us never fear to negotiate." If you don't ask, you won't get. Negotiating your salary and your departure are the most important negotiations with your employer. Make sure to get the first one right to set the stage for the rest of your career with your new employer.

Salary Negotiation: 33 Things to Negotiate Other than Money
By: *Jorg Stegemann, 26 Jan 2015,*
Kennedy Executive Search & Outplacement

Chapter 11: Exit Strategy and Career Maintenance

Whether candidates already have new jobs or have decided to quit without one, how they resign matters—and it may even affect them for the rest of their careers. Many people fail to recognize the importance of the explicit and implicit messages they send when they resign. This is the time to build—not burn—bridges. What is communicated will be remembered. No matter what the experience on the job has been, now is the time to create a positive picture of that experience and the value of those relationships.

First Things First—Put It in Writing

It is advantageous to resign with a letter that formally documents the decision. Not only is this considerate, it also provides protection. It creates legal documentation of the departure date, appropriate notice, and voluntary separation from the company. The letter should be written to the immediate boss, be as short as possible, and include relevant factual data. It should also include a "statement of appreciation" about the opportunity with the company. It's important to keep a copy.

Put a Pretty Face on It

If this has been a good job and the candidate is leaving for a better one, the goal is for everyone to be happy for the departing employee. If this was not a good job, no matter how awful it was, the goal is still for everyone to be happy for the departing person.

The easiest starting point is to let the employer know:
- This decision received serious thought (and perhaps that it was a difficult decision).
- The opportunity and experience with the organization (company, department) is appreciated.
- The relationships that were built are valued.

Speak genuinely and from the heart. Even if it was the worst boss ever, it is still true that a lot was learned—even if it was only how *not* to manage a project or how *not* to treat people. The best way for people to be happy for the departing employee is to make them feel valued and appreciated. What? You say you worked for Attila the Hun? If someone asks about the experience, say something along the lines of, "It was an experience I'll never forget," or "I learned a lot about territory expansion."

The act of resigning is not the time to be angry about past experiences or to be used as an opportunity to vent about all the things that are wrong with the company, the job, or the people there. Guess what? No one cares. And leaving scorched earth behind has a way of coming back around.

Parting Is Such Sweet Sorrow . . . or Is It?

It should be clear by now that people's careers are in their own hands. "Free agents" have to learn how to effectively represent themselves throughout their careers—in, out, up, down, and sideways. While many people who have, for very good reasons, stayed at the same company for 20 years, these days that type of longevity is more likely to be viewed as a negative rather than as a positive by recruiters and hiring managers. The three important messages about leaving a job or company are:
1. Planning ahead in terms of when and how you will leave is more essential than ever.
2. When it comes to leaving, there are guidelines that will increase your chances of success.
3. Don't burn bridges.

Exiting as a Career Strategy

Today, developing a strategy for leaving a job is almost as important as developing a strategy for finding one. Companies simply don't guarantee lifetime employment anymore. A couple of decades ago, employees could count on being employed by Papa Company from "cradle to grave." Those days are long gone. In today's fiercely competitive global economy more organizations than ever are downsizing, right-sizing, reorganizing, outsourcing, off-shoring, and merging in order to stay alive. In this atmosphere no one's job is safe.

In addition, companies are often less involved in career planning, promotional tracking, and directing employees' advancement. Individuals must take responsibility for their own growth and career success. What that means, then, is that no matter what job or aspirations are held, it is crucial to always have an exit strategy planned.

There are a few specific situations where a coach can help a client create a defined, intentional exit strategy. Here are some examples of how that coaching conversation might take place.

- **Newly hired college graduates who want to return to school for an advanced degree down the road.** Most top-notch business graduate schools prefer candidates who have worked for at least a couple of years. To that end, if you take a job right after receiving your undergraduate degree and know for sure that you want to get your MBA or equivalent, you should have a specific strategy in mind sooner rather than later. Many companies offer generous tuition reimbursement programs when you're ready to go back to school. Working out your exit or transition plan ahead of time may allow you to capitalize on your company's support and post-degree opportunities. Handled properly, you can also retain the goodwill of your employer when you depart.

- **Someone who has agreed to take a "development job" in order to learn or improve valuable new skills, but the job does not fit their natural talents or professional "sweet spots."** These can be important career growth opportunities, but the danger is getting stuck in a job where you are never going to be great. Your stress level will probably be higher, your performance reviews could suffer, and the potential growth opportunity could, in fact, derail your otherwise stellar track record. In these situations, you should negotiate terms and conditions, specifically how and when you will transition out, before you take the gig.

- **A working environment or boss that is just plain toxic.** This happens far too often at companies with cutthroat cultures, unenlightened leadership, or an obsession with short-term performance. Sometimes, you just have to get out. If your working environment or boss is taking a serious toll on your morale, satisfaction, or health . . . RUN! However, be smart about it and don't burn any bridges. In most cases you'll be more successful in your transition if you don't pull the rip cord right away in anger or panic. Instead, find a way to handle the immediate stressors so you can bide your time, maybe several months, while you put together a viable, realistic, and achievable exit strategy. You may find opportunities in other parts of the same company where you can escape the poison of your current situation. Or, you may have to leave the company altogether.

Tips for Exit-Ready Career Management

Leaving a job, company, department, or position is normal these days. In fact, it's pervasive. Here are a few important tips when exiting, but typically aren't emphasized or executed well. Way too many people ignore, are naïve about, or fall short in handling these simple elements.

- Have a current resume—update it every year.

- Keep track of accomplishments so they can be included accurately on the resume and talked about in interviews.

- Build a robust network of connections and keep it fresh. The best time to build it is when it isn't needed. Refresh relationships with people from the past. If they're still alive, they're a networking contact.

- Continuously expand your skills and credentials.

- Constantly scan the horizon for what's happening in the industry, community, and the field.

- Keep all critical documents, such as recommendation letters, awards, certificates, diplomas, articles, and media coverage, in one place. A handy 3-ring binder works well as a career portfolio. Or, scan the important documents and save them electronically in a career portfolio.

Jobs, companies, and whole industries are fluid these days. The best strategies for companies and for careers require adaptability—there is no way to predict the game-changing events that can emerge in an instant. So having a career plan in place that includes a variety of pathways to achieve ultimate professional goals will provide peace of mind and self-confidence to handle any curve balls.

Ongoing Career Success and Maintenance

Intentional career management sets a professional on a path of self-determination. Here are a few critical concepts for successful intentional career management.

1. There is a difference between having a mentor and a sponsor. Both are useful, but they serve different purposes. A mentor is the wise Yoda—they can share from their experiences, offer advice as needed, and provide support and guidance as requested; they expect very little in return. Sponsors, on the other hand, are more invested in the success of the professional and use their influence to help them gain visibility and advancement within the company.

2. It is important, if not essential, to continuously build skills. The term "Lego Careers" describes putting lots of pieces together in different combinations to maximize a person's value. Some of these include:

    - Individual development plans (IDPs)
    - Career advancing short-term assignments or project
    - Targeted training, especially programs that deliver valuable certifications, degrees, or coveted skills
    - Personal PR plans for gaining visibility, internally and externally
    - Experience in broad functional or diverse organizational areas

3. **Continue to network.** Regular and strategic networking is part of any professional job. Whether content in a job, looking for advancement, or keeping doors open for future opportunities, networking has to be considered a vital part of any management or professional job. It doesn't stop when a new job is secured. It continues for the entirety of a career. It has to be something that is intentional and systematic. Plan some time, a few hours, on a regular basis, once a quarter or more, and block it out on the calendar. Without a system or discipline like this, it can easily drop off the radar and not kept current until the next new job shift is pending. Networking is forever—embrace it, have fun, and reap the rewards!

Closing

Now that you have worked your way thought this workbook, it might be helpful to make specific notations about the areas that 1) you will use most in your business, 2) you want to learn at a deeper level, and 3) areas you would like to research more.

Career Coaching is unquestionably going to be around for a very long time. And your ability to capitalize on this segment of the market can add significant value to your clients and contribute to your long-term coaching success. As the world of career coaching continues to evolve, your investment in acquiring these skills provides a solid foundation for your future growth.

Notes: _____

_____

_____

_____

_____

_____

_____

_____

_____

_____

_____

_____

_____

_____

_____

_____

_____

_____

_____

_____

_____

_____

_____

Notes: _____

_____

_____

_____

_____

_____

_____

_____

_____

_____

_____

_____

_____

_____

_____

_____

_____

_____

_____

_____

_____

_____

_____

_____

_____

_____

_____

_____

_____

_____

_____

_____

_____

_____

_____

APPENDIX

Books for Reference

Books	Author/Source
The Coaching Bible	Ian McDermott & Wendy Jago
Finding Your Perfect Work: The New Career Guide to Making a Living, Creating a Life	Paul & Sarah Edwards
Coach Yourself to Success	Talane Miedaner
You Already Know How to Be Great	Alan Fine
Do What You Are	Paul D. Tieger & Barbara Barron-Tieger
What Got You Here Won't Get You There	Marshall Goldsmith
Making a Life, Making a Living: Reclaiming Your Purpose and Passion in Business and in Life	Mark Albion
To Sell Is Human: The Surprising Truth About Moving Others	Daniel Pink
Antifragile: Things That Gain From Disorder	Nassim Nicholas Taleb
The New Geography of Jobs	Enrico Moretti
Be Smart	Paula Asinof & Mina Brown
Be Sharp (including Spanish edition)	Paula Asinof & Mina Brown
Yellow Brick Path Recommended Books	www.yellowbrickpath.com/books

Websites

Organization	Website
International Coach Federation (ICF)	www.coachfederation.org
World Business and Executive Coach Summit (WBECS)	www.wbecs.com
Worldwide Association of Business Coaches	www.wabccoaches.com
International Association of Coaching	www.certifiedcoach.org
Career Directors International	www.careerdirectors.com
Career Thought Leaders	www.careerthoughtleaders.com
Yellow Brick Path	www.yellowbrickpath.com
Positive Coach LLC	www.positivecoach.com
Coach Academy International	www.coachacademyinternational.com

Sample External Prospect Information Form— Prequalification

Client Name	
Date	
Referred By	
Referral Fee?	
Individual/Corp	
Title/Function	
Company	
Compensation Range (optional)	
Situation/Need	
Next Steps	
Fee Quoted	
Contact Info	

COMMENTS:

Scheduled Time(s)	

Sample Client Profile

Name: _____

Company: _____

Title: _____

Brief description of your job: _____

Email address: _____

Mailing address: _____

Home address: _____

Business phone: _____   Mobile phone: _____

Home phone: _____   Fax: _____

Home Email: _____   Birthday (month, day): _____

Name of Admin: _____   Admin's phone: _____

Other information relevant to our coaching: _____

_____

Credit Card Information

Credit Card Type	Visa___ MasterCard___ American Express___ Discover____	
Credit Card Number		
Credit Card Expiration Date		Security Code:
Customer Name *Exactly as on the Card*		
Company Name		
Billing Address		
Phone number		
Email address (for receipt)		

Sample Email for Follow up Referrals

To: [Coach], [Prospect]

From: [Referrer]

Subject: [Prospect Name]

[Prospect Name], as discussed, please contact [Coach] [Coach phone number], [Coach email address]. More information about [Coach] can be found at [Coach's website].

[Short description of coach's area of expertise]. [Programs and pricing information as applicable and appropriate.]

[Coach], I have suggested [Prospect Name], [Prospect phone number], [Prospect email address] contact you. [Brief description about Prospect, needs, background information, as applicable and appropriate.]

[Referrer regular email signature]

Sample Client Coaching Agreement (Yellow Brick Path)

Coach's Credentials: *The coach's credentials detailed (who the client has hired)*

Client Fully Responsible: As a client, I understand and agree that I am fully responsible for my physical, mental, and emotional well-being during coaching sessions, including my choices, decisions, and actions. I am aware that I can choose to discontinue coaching at any time. I also understand that I am also responsible for final proofreading of and making or arranging for correction to any documents, such as resumes.

Coaching Boundaries: I understand coaching does not involve the diagnosis or treatment of mental disorders. Although from time to time we may touch on topics outside the coach's areas of expertise, such information or opinion is not a substitute for professional advice by legal, medical, financial, business, spiritual, or other qualified professionals.

Confidentiality: I understand that information will be held confidential to Yellow Brick Path, its staff and service providers, unless I state otherwise in writing, except under very specific circumstances such as illegal activity, a valid court order or subpoena, imminent or likely risk of danger to yourself or others. I understand that coaches are not covered by "privilege" in a court of law. I understand that information may be *anonymously and hypothetically* shared with others for training or consultation.

I give permission to YBP to confer with the following other people about my coaching:
Name: _____
Name: _____

If I engage YBP or its associates to assist in development of my LinkedIn profile, I authorize them to access my profile and make changes to it on my behalf for these purposes.

Fees and Payments: Unless otherwise arranged, I understand that fees are payable in advance. I also understand that fees include a non-refundable deposit to be applied to total fees. I will forfeit the deposit in the event of cancellation or for "no shows". I also understand YBP charges an additional fee equal to the deposit amount for re-scheduling with less than 24 *business* hours' notice (e.g. Monday 1 pm for Tuesday 1 pm or Friday 1 pm for Monday 1 pm). Unused non-refundable deposits may be applied to services for up to 1 year from the date of payment.

I understand that my paid session starts at the scheduled appointment time. Any dispute regarding services *is limited to* fees paid, cancellation of unpaid charges invoiced, and/or cancellation of additional contracted services, with the amount and terms to be agreed upon by the parties. I understand that from time to time, my coach may refer people to other coaches or other professionals and also may obtain referrals from others, some of which involve arrangements by which referral fees are paid.

Mailing List: I agree to have my name and contact information added to the Yellow Brick Path mailing list to receive newsletters and information about Yellow Brick Path events and products. Yellow Brick Path mailing lists are not sold or provided to third parties. Opt out: _____ [initials]

I have read and agree to the above.

Client Contact Information:

Name:	
Address:	
City/ST/ZIP:	
Telephone:	
Email:	

Client Signature: _____   **Date** _____

Resumes & Bios Infographic

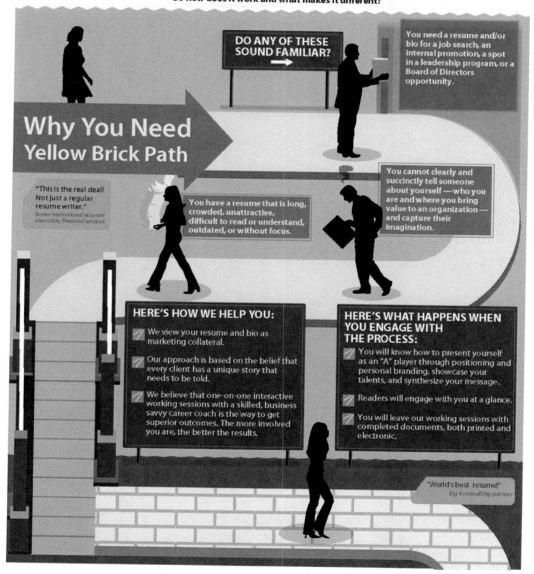

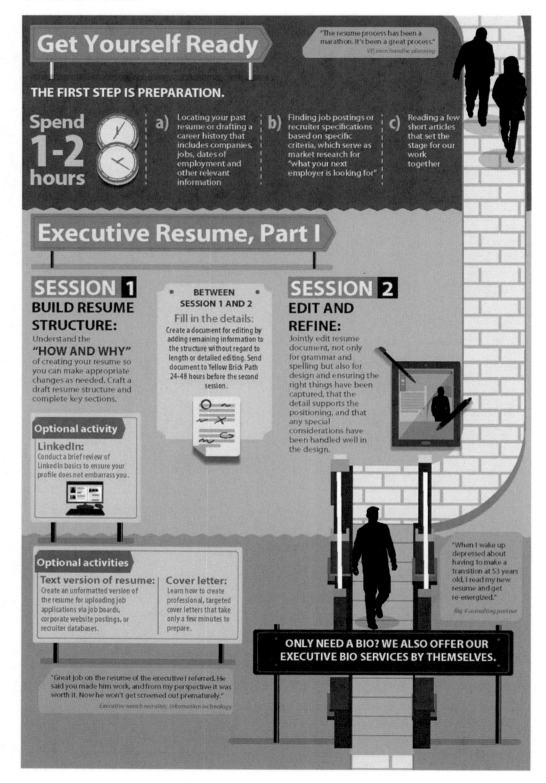

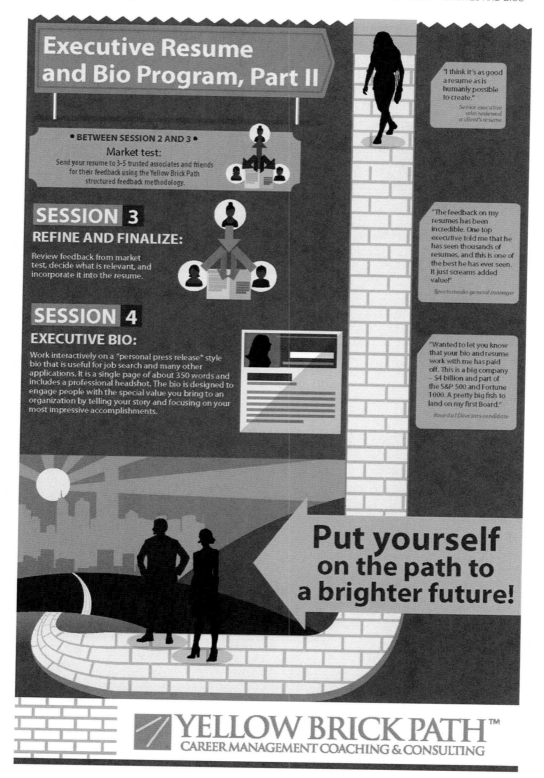

Resume Template

NAME
City, State
Address
Available to Travel (50% or more) and/or Relocate [Globally]
Languages, Security, Shift, Citizenship, Education/Certification in Process, etc. (if applicable to next job)

Phone: Email:
LinkedIn URL

HEADLINE
Subhead

Positioning: This is where the positioning section goes. It helps you talk more articulately about yourself when asked the question "Tell Me about Yourself". It is also important for Executive Bios. This is where the positioning section goes. It helps you talk more articulately about yourself when asked the question "Tell Me about Yourself". It is also important for Executive Bios. This is where the positioning section goes. It helps you talk more articulately about yourself when asked the question "Tell Me about Yourself".

Keyword (Functional Skills)
Technology or Other Appropriate Sub-line
Keyword (Personal Characteristics)

COMPANY, Location (EXC:ABC)	**website**	**Dates**

Company description

Position Title
Job description
- Accomplishment
- Accomplishment

COMPANY, City, ST	**website**	**Dates**

Company description

Position Title, Location (dates)
Job description
- Accomplishment
- Accomplishment

Position Title, Location (dates)
Job description
- Accomplishment
- Accomplishment

EARLIER CAREER
Held positions

EDUCATION
CERTIFICATIONS & LICENSES
PROFESSIONAL AFFILIATIONS
COMMMUNITY ACTIVITIES
LANGUAGES
MEDIA COVERAGE/PUBLICATIONS/SPEAKING ENGAGEMENTS
MILITARY
ARTS & ATHLETICS ACHIEVEMENTS

Sample Resume

JOHN MENDOZA, CPA

Milwaukee, WI – Available to Travel and/or Relocate

4221 Marketplace Road, Shorewood, WI 99999

Fluent in English & Spanish

Phone: 444.555.6666   Email: john.mendoza@email.com

www.linkedin.com/etc

SENIOR FINANCIAL EXECUTIVE

Manufacturing and Distribution

Innovative and strategic financial leader. Expertise in strategic investments and operational projects, primarily in the U.S. and Latin American markets. Called on to lead complex corporate programs leveraging his broad experience base and consultative communication style. Counsels teams on better operational and market execution and provides insight to the Board of Directors and executive team on sound business and financial approaches. Integrally involved in determining investor communication strategy and managing the analyst call process.

Global Strategy – M&A – Risk Management – Technology Oversight

"Big Four" Audit Experience

ROI Focused – Metrics Driven – Proactive Decision Maker – Team Builder – Articulate

---

AMERICAN CORPORATION (NYSE:ACO)   **www.amcorp.com**   **2001 – Present**

$350 million dollar, global manufacturer and distributor of specialty polymer composite materials and components to growing markets around the world. Products are based on core technologies in polymers, fillers and adhesion

Corporate Controller – Corporate Officer, Milwaukee, WI

Manage all public and internal financial and operational reporting, strategic planning and capital administration, financial system implementations and administration, M&A, operation initiatives, and financial service functions. Direct management of 25 corporate finance staff and oversight of over 50 worldwide operational finance professionals.

- Led the successful acquisition and integration of multiple companies ranging from $15 to $85 million in annual revenues. Also led the divestiture of a $35 million nonstrategic business and the start up of an India-based $25 million joint venture
- Led the team that successfully established a $50 million manufacturing and distribution center in Mexico – from Board approval through the start up of operations
- Eliminated over $1.5 million in corporate overhead through streamlining of consolidated reporting systems and processes and improving quality (accuracy, integrity, timeliness) of the executive financial and operational reporting model
- Generated over $5 million in productivity gains by playing a key role in the successful launch of Six Sigma within the organization

MAXIMUM INDUSTRIES (NYSE:MSM)   **www.maximumind.com**   **1998 – 2001**

$4 billion dollar company that manufactures and sells a wide range of electrical and tools products

Division Controller – Tools Division, Los Angeles, CA (1999-2001)

Managed all financial and tax reporting, financial analysis, budget and capital administration, treasury, financial support functions, and internal control administration for the $950 million Tools Division. Direct management of 25 division financial staff and oversight of 200 financial staff within the division operations.

- Drove $1 million in savings from headcount reduction, process streamlining, and system rationalization in leading the reorganization as the company consolidated two divisions
- Completed numerous multi-million dollar strategic initiatives by providing financial project management in acquisitions and integration, operational restructuring, and asset dispositions

Corporate Audit, Senior Manager, Chicago, IL (1998-1999)

Teamed with management in identifying critical business risks and developing innovative business solutions including new ERP system implementations, major joint venture investments in Brazil, new acquisitions, plant expansions/rationalizations, and Corporate reporting

- Reduced audit budget by over $500,000 by redirecting focus to business risk and developed new assurance service tools to deploy the new business risk philosophy
- Instrumental in the $7 million reduction of the purchase price of a major acquisition through due diligence and careful evaluation of market conditions

GMPK INTERNATIONAL   www.gmpk.com   1991 – 1998
Largest global public accounting firm

Audit Manager, Miami, FL (1997-1998)
Assistant Audit Manager, Mexico City, Mexico (1994-1996)
Supervising Senior Accountant, Miami, FL (1991-1994)
Managed a diverse multinational client base in manufacturing, retail and distribution including a $3 billion publicly traded, global, world-class supplier of power generation equipment and services
- Led the office's first outsourcing of a major client's internal audit function which produced a 25% annual savings for the company and $2 million of incremental revenue for the firm
- Established a firm wide reputation for expertise in the Mexican accounting practices and statutory reporting regulations

EDUCATION & CERTIFICATIONS
MS Accounting, University of Florida, 1994
BBA, Magna cum Laude, University of South Florida, 1990
CPA, State of Florida, 1991

LANGUAGES: Fluent in English and Spanish

Sample Resume in Text Format

```
JOHN MENDOZA, CPA
Milwaukee, WI - Available to Travel and/or Relocate
4221 Marketplace Road
Shorewood, WI 99999

Fluent in English & Spanish

Phone: 444.555.6666
Email: john.mendoza@email.com
www.linkedin.com/etc


SUMMARY PROFILE

SENIOR FINANCIAL EXECUTIVE
Manufacturing and Distribution

Innovative and strategic financial leader. Expertise in strategic investments
and operational projects, primarily in the U.S. and Latin American markets.
Called on to lead complex corporate programs leveraging his broad experience
base and consultative communication style. Counsels teams on better
operational and market execution and provides insight to the Board of
Directors and executive team on sound business and financial approaches.
Integrally involved in determining investor communication strategy and
managing the analyst call process.

GLOBAL STRATEGY - M&A - RISK MANAGEMENT - TECHNOLOGY OVERSIGHT
"Big Four" Audit Experience

ROI FOCUSED - METRICS DRIVEN - PROACTIVE DECISION MAKER - TEAM BUILDER -
ARTICULATE


EXPERIENCE

AMERICAN CORPORATION (NYSE:ACO)
www.amcorp.com
2001 - Present
$350 million dollar, global manufacturer and distributor of specialty polymer
composite materials and components to growing markets around the world.
Products are based on core technologies in polymers, fillers and adhesion

CORPORATE CONTROLLER - CORPORATE OFFICER, MILWAUKEE, WI
Manage all public and internal financial and operational reporting, strategic
planning and capital administration, financial system implementations and
administration, M&A, operation initiatives, and financial service functions.
Direct management of 25 corporate finance staff and oversight of over 50
worldwide operational finance professionals.
-Led the successful acquisition and integration of multiple companies ranging
from $15 to $85 million in annual revenues. Also led the divestiture of a $35
million nonstrategic business and the start up of an India-based $25 million
joint venture
-Led the team that successfully established a $50 million manufacturing and
distribution center in Mexico - from Board approval through the start up of
operations
-Eliminated over $1.5 million in corporate overhead through streamlining of
```

1

consolidated reporting systems and processes and improving quality (accuracy, integrity, timeliness) of the executive financial and operational reporting model
-Generated over $5 million in productivity gains by playing a key role in the successful launch of Six Sigma within the organization

MAXIMUM INDUSTRIES (NYSE:MSM)
www.maximumind.com
1998 - 2001
$4 billion dollar company that manufactures and sells a wide range of electrical and tools products

DIVISION CONTROLLER - TOOLS DIVISION, LOS ANGELES, CA (1999-2001)
Managed all financial and tax reporting, financial analysis, budget and capital administration, treasury, financial support functions, and internal control administration for the $950 million Tools Division. Direct management of 25 division financial staff and oversight of 200 financial staff within the division operations.
-Drove $1 million in savings from headcount reduction, process streamlining, and system rationalization in leading the reorganization as the company consolidated two divisions
-Completed numerous multi-million dollar strategic initiatives by providing financial project management in acquisitions and integration, operational restructuring, and asset dispositions

CORPORATE AUDIT, SENIOR MANAGER, CHICAGO, IL (1998-1999)
Teamed with management in identifying critical business risks and developing innovative business solutions including new ERP system implementations, major joint venture investments in Brazil, new acquisitions, plant expansions/rationalizations, and Corporate reporting
-Reduced audit budget by over $500,000 by redirecting focus to business risk and developed new assurance service tools to deploy the new business risk philosophy
-Instrumental in the $7 million reduction of the purchase price of a major acquisition through due diligence and careful evaluation of market conditions

GMPK INTERNATIONAL
www.gmpk.com
1991 - 1998
Largest global public accounting firm

AUDIT MANAGER, MIAMI, FL (1997-1998)
ASSISTANT AUDIT MANAGER, MEXICO CITY, MEXICO (1994-1996)
SUPERVISING SENIOR ACCOUNTANT, MIAMI, FL (1991-1994)
Managed a diverse multinational client base in manufacturing, retail and distribution including a $3 billion publicly traded, global, world-class supplier of power generation equipment and services
-Led the office's first outsourcing of a major client's internal audit function which produced a 25% annual savings for the company and $2 million of incremental revenue for the firm
-Established a firm wide reputation for expertise in the Mexican accounting practices and statutory reporting regulations

2

EDUCATION & CERTIFICATIONS
MS Accounting, University of Florida, 1994
BBA, Magna cum Laude, University of South Florida, 1990
CPA, State of Florida, 1991

LANGUAGES: Fluent in English and Spanish

3

Sample New Grad Resume - Basic

RAJ PRADIP
13531 N. Oak Street, Apt. 9B
Seattle, WA 99999

Phone: 999-999-9999
Email: raj.pradip@email.com
www.linkedin.com/rajpradip

SUMMARY
Pharmacy Technician
Certificate Expected December 2015

- Learns quickly
- Well-organized
- Strong work ethic

- Team player
- Good communication skills
- 5 years prior work experience

Pharmacy Operations – Drug Dispensing – IV Preparation – Chemotherapy – Compounding
CPR Certified – OSHA and HIPAA Training Certificate

EDUCATION

ALLIED HEALTH COLLEGE, Seattle, WA www.ahcseattle.com **Certificate 12/2015**
AHC provides high quality, post-secondary programs of education in Allied Healthcare. Division of New Schools Corporation. Accredited by ABHES and ACICS.

Pharmacy Technology Program: *720 hours lecture and lab; 180 hours externship*
Medical terminology, human structure and function, pharmacology mathematics, pharmaceutical safety, pharmacy computer applicant, fundamental techniques, and advanced techniques.
- Cumulative GPA 3.9 (President's List/Top Honors)
- Perfect Attendance

ABC COMMUNITY COLLEGE, Redmond, WA **2009 – 2010**
General Studies and Basic Science **30 semester hours**

EXPERIENCE

DAZZLE COMPANY, Seattle, WA **2/2013 – 1/2015**
National jewelry retailer chain
Sales Associate
Sold fine jewelry to customers, including specialty items. Recognized for outstanding sales by twice being named employee of the month.

HIGH LIFE, INC., Redmond, WA **1/2010 – 2/2013**
Manufactured and sold high-end costume jewelry in franchised retail outlets
Supervisor, ABC Mall Location (1/2012 – 2/2013)
Managed a team of 3 sales associates who staffed a mall-corridor jewelry kiosk. Opened and closed operations.

Sales Associate (1/2010 – 1/2012)

Sample New Grad Resume - Standard

KEISHA MORGAN
Providence, RI – Available to Travel and/or Relocate Globally
9876 Little Street, Barrington, RI 99999
Fluent Mandarin Chinese

Phone: 888.989.8989   Email: keisahmorgan@email.com
www.linkedin.com/keishamorgan

INTERNATIONAL MARKETING
Willing to travel and relocate

Passionate about marketing in the fashion, home accessory, and "green" industries. Intuitive sense of trends, consumer tastes, and "what's going to be in". Adaptable and flexible. Enjoy international travel and comfortable in diverse cultures.

EDUCATION and INTERNSHIP
BA, Markets and Culture, Kingpin University, 2007
As one of KU's newest majors, this multidisciplinary program focuses on the changing economic and social practices shape the world's markets. The dynamics of markets and the factors influence production, distribution, and consumption in the U.S. and globally are examined from many perspectives.

STUDY ABROAD – Summer 2005
Nankai University, Tianjim, China – Beginning Mandarin Chinese
Suzhou University, Suzhou, China – Chinese History and Culture
The Good Roots Project, Bagio, Philippines – Environmental and Cultural Anthropology

DINO, INC., Boston, MA   **www.dino.com**   **9/2003 – 12/2003**
$1.2 billion global design, marketing and distribution company specializing in consumer fashion accessories sold to department stores, specialty retail stores and through the Company's website in the U.S. and 90 countries.
  Marketing Intern
  Designed quarterly executive summaries of media product placements. Managed international and domestic correspondence. Worked on cross-functional projects with advertising, art, and human resources.

CAMPUS LEADERSHIP
President, KU's Environmental Society, 2006 – 2007
eWomen Network International Conference – VIP Coordinator, 2006

PROFESSIONAL EXPERIENCE
THE BEJIN NEW ORIENTAL FOREIGN LANGUAGE SCHOOOL   **8/2007 – 11/2007**
Yangzhou, China
One of the top K-12 residential schools for Chinese students aspiring to college education and professional careers

  Teacher – 2nd Grade English
  In charge of 5 classes of 25 students each. Excellent performance feedback from Vice Principal and Director of Foreign Teachers for student classroom interaction, creative lesson plans, and communication skills.

OTHER WORK EXPERIENCE
UNIVERSITY PUBLIC LIBRARY, Barrington, RI   **7/2006 – 8/2007**
Circulation Desk Coordinator

UNITY CHURCH OF PROVIDENCE, Dallas, TX   **1/2003 – 8/2005**
Assistant to Project and Business Managers

Sample New Grad Resume - Experienced

JOAN ROBERTS
Available to Relocate
1234 Main Street, Arlington, VA 99999
Executive MBA, Top Dog University (TDU)
Phone: 222.333.4444   Email: joanroberts@email.com
www.linkedin.com/joanroberts

COMMERCIAL PROCESS MANAGEMENT
Cross-Functional Solutions – Process Development

Creative, forward-thinking leader who thrives on crafting new products and services, especially ones that take advantage of technology to create efficiencies. A mentor who brings out the best in people and creates high performance sales teams by building a culture of fun and success. Resourceful and knowledgeable about where to go to get things done. Grounded in analytics and delivered with an upbeat, confident, and approachable style, recognized as the person who will "make it happen".

Strategy & Plan Development – Sales/Marketing Management – Financial Analysis – Team Leadership
Advanced Excel and PowerPoint – Project Management

Relationship Builder – Analytic – Mentor/Coach – Technologically Proficient

EDUCATION

Executive MBA, Top Dog University (TDU), 2014
TDU Executive MBA program ranks #5 in the world by Bloomberg Businessweek (2013), #15 in the U.S. by U.S. News and World Report (2014), and #22 in the world by The Economist (2013)
GPA: 3.5

COURSES INCLUDED
Business Strategy – Marketing Strategy – Entrepreneurship – Negotiation
Global Business Environment – Mergers & Acquisitions
Foundation in Accounting & Finance, Economics, Law, Operations Research & Statistics, Organization Behavior

INTERNATIONAL STUDY - CHINA
Two-week program visiting and studying American corporations that have commenced operations in China with emphasis on understanding emerging markets. Companies included Caterpillar, Dell, GE, and 7-Eleven.

BS, Accounting, Superior College, 2004

LAKEPOINT, Arlington, VA   **www.lakepoint.com**   **2006 – Present**
From startup in 2005, grown into a premier nationwide provider of telecommunications and other home services based on an innovative direct selling strategy. Currently 14th largest direct selling company in the world and consistently ranked on the Direct Selling News Global 100 List as a top-tier company.

Director of New Products (2014 – Present)
Lead the evaluation of potential new verticals outside of core product lines and determine how they fit into current product offerings and sales strategies. Responsible for vetting new concepts, evaluating vendors, and running pilot programs. Also design business processes, manage product testing, prepare business cases, evaluate profitability and scalability, and forecast P&L.

- Launched the Company's 1st non-commodity based product offering – credit monitoring, identity protection and technical support – that sets the stage for strategic diversification and was profitable in the 1st month
- Utilizing a 3rd party underwriter, launched alternate method of enrollment that reduces the cost to the consumer without creating risk for the Company

Director of Commercial Sales & Service (2010 – 2014)
Manager of Commercial Sales & Service (2007 – 2010)
Recruited, trained, developed, and motivated team of sales representatives into a cohesive team. Led 20-person team in improving sales performance, achieving goals, and accomplishing Company objectives. Analyzed and calculated monthly agent commissions.

Sales

- Led the team that delivered $270 million in revenue for the firm from 2008 – 2013 accounting for 10% of the Company's revenues
- Led the team that closed 5,300 deals in 2012, a Company record
- Drove the design of 2 CRM platforms, one organically developed and the other using Microsoft Dynamics, that evaluated current sales processes and streamlined them to increase the speed to sell

Service

- Instrumental in the Company being ranked #2 in the commercial telecommunicationsindustry in satisfaction in Texas by JD Powers and Associates in 2009 and 2010 (JD Powers stopped doing Commercial rankings after 2010)
- Increased service performance by consolidating customer Service and Operations into a single group of highly skilled "super agents"

Commercial Sales Agent (2006 – 2007)
Commercial Operations Analyst (2006)
Negotiated commercial telecommunications contracts with customers as well as verified accuracy of commercial telecommunication contracts received from 3rd party sales organization. Once verified, processed enrollment transactions for the completed 3rd party contracts. Served as the billing and transactional expert for Customer Service Department for all commercial accounts.

CENTRAL MUTUAL, Dallas, TX   **www.centralmutual.com**   **2003 – 2006**
Offers a comprehensive approach to financial security solutions including life insurance, long-term care insurance, disability income insurance, annuities, investment products, and advisory products and services.
  Financial Representative (Sales)
Built a practice from the ground up and generated a book of business through networking and referrals
- Achieved *First 40* new agent sales achievement
- Achieved 57 weeks of continuous production measured by sales closed

PROFESSIONAL & COMMUNITY AFFILIATIONS
Direct Sales Association
Minneapolis Young Professionals
TDU Alumni Association
Assistant Coach (7th & 8th grades), St. Margaret Catholic Preparatory School

LANGUAGES
Conversational Spanish

SPEAKING ENGAGEMENTS
Regular speaker at Lakepoint's Annual Sales Conference addressing audiences of up to 3,500 sales associates

Bio Template

FIRSTNAME LASTNAME

Title (or Tag Line)
Company (or Area of Speciality)

Keywords
Secondary Keywords

BOARD/INDUSTRY EXPERIENCE (Section Optional)
Company/Organization
Descriptor
Company/Organization
Descriptor

FIRSTNAME LASTNAME Positioning Lorem ipsum sed dolor sit amet, consectetuer adipiscing elit, sed diam nonummy nibh euismod tincidunt ut laoreet dolore magna aliquam erat volutpat. Ut wisi enim ad minim veniam, quis nostrud exerci tation ullamcorper suscipit lobortis nisl ut aliquip ex ea commodo consequat. Duis autem vel eum iriure dolor in hendrerit in vulputate velit esse molestie dolore eu feugiat nulla facilisis at vero eros et accumsan et euismod tincidunt ut laoreet dolore magna aliquam erat volutpat. Ut wisi enim ad minim veniam, quis nostrud exerci tation ullamcorper suscipit lobortis nisl ut aliquip ex ea commodo.

Current Position Lorem ipsum dolor sit amet, consectetuer adipiscing elit, sed diam nonummy nibh euismod tincidunt ut laoreet dolore magna aliquam erat volutpat. Ut wisi enim ad minim veniam, quis nostrud exerci tation ullamcorper suscipit lobortis nisl ut aliquip ex ea commodo consequat. Duis autem vel eum iriure dolor in hendrerit. euismod tincidunt ut laoreet dolore magna aliquam erat volutpat. Ut wisi enim ad minim veniam, quis nostrud exerci tation ullamcorper suscipit lobortis nisl ut aliquip ex ea commodo consequat. Duis autem vel eum iriure dolor in hendrerit. Ut wisi enim ad minim veniam, quis nostrud exerci tation ullamcorper suscipit lobortis nisl ut aliquip ex ea commodo.

Rest of Career Lorem ipsum dolor sit amet, consectetuer adipiscing elit, sed diam nonummy nibh euismod tincidunt ut laoreet dolore magna aliquam erat volutpat. Ut wisi enim ad minim veniam, quis nostrud exerci tation ullamcorper suscipit lobortis nisl ut aliquip ex ea commodo consequat. Duis autem vel eum iriure. euismod tincidunt ut laoreet dolore magna aliquam erat volutpat. Ut wisi enim ad minim veniam, quis nostrud exerci tation ullamcorper suscipit lobortis nisl ut aliquip ex ea commodo consequat. Duis autem vel eum iriure dolor in hendrerit.

Credentials Lorem ipsum dolor sit amet, consectetuer adipiscing elit, sed diam nonummy nibh euismod tincidunt ut laoreet dolore magna aliquam erat volutpat. Ut wisi enim ad minim veniam, quis nostrud exerci tation ullamcorper suscipit lobortis nisl ut aliquip ex ea commodo. Ut wisi enim ad minim veniam, quis nostrud exerci tation ullamcorper suscipit lobortis nisl ut aliquip ex ea commodo.

Phone   **Email**

Sample Bio

John Mendoza, CPA

Corporate Controller & Corporate Officer
American Corporation

Global Manufacturing — Strategy – Risk Management
M&A — Technology Oversight

JOHN MENDOZA is an innovative and strategic financial leader with expertise in strategic investments and operational projects, primarily in the U.S. and Latin American markets. He is often called on to lead complex corporate programs leveraging his broad experience base and consultative communication style. John counsels teams on better operational and market execution and provides insight to the Board of Directors and executive team on sound business and financial approaches. He is also integrally involved in determining investor communication strategy and managing the analyst call process.

Currently, as Corporate Controller and Corporate Officer for American Corporation, a publicly held global manufacturer and distributor of specialty materials, John manages all financial operations worldwide, including the financial aspects of M&A initiatives. In this role, he led the team that successfully established a $50 million manufacturing campus in Mexico – from Board approval through the start up. He also helped generate over $6.5 million in productivity gains by playing a key role in the successful launch of Six Sigma and by streamlining consolidated reporting systems.

Previously, as Division Controller at Maximum Industries, he drove $1 million in savings from headcount reduction and system rationalizations in leading a reorganization of the finance team. He also served as a Senior Audit Manager where he reduced the audit budget over $500,000 by redirecting focus to business risk and developing more efficient audit tools. He began his career at GMPK International where he rose to the position of Audit Manager. While at GMPK, he spent two years in Mexico City gaining financial reporting expertise in Latin American business environments.

John is a CPA. He holds a BBA, Magna cum Laude, from the University of South Florida and an MS in Accounting from the University of Florida. He is fluent in English and Spanish.

444.555.6666   john.mendoza@email.com

Cover Letter Template

NAME
Address
City ST ZIP
Phone   Email

Date

Name
Title
Company
Address (or email or phone)
City, ST ZIP

Dear (Name or Title) (title may be "Recruiter")

Purpose of contact and statement of contribution. . .
I am writing because (referred by, posting response, other purpose)
I will be (asset to, strong contributor, etc.) to (personalize to the company and job)

Qualifications and alignment with the job. . .
Excellent match/fit for position (if have spec – and meet most)
- Bullet 1
- Bullet 2
- Bullet 3
- Bullet 4

Special considerations/Credentials. . .
In addition, (willing to relocate, travel, language, education, etc.)

Follow up. . .
Look forward to talking further, resume (and cover letter) attached, cell phone and/or email

Sincerely,

Signature

Name

Sample Cover Letter

JOHN MENDOZA, CPA
4221 Marketplace Road
Shorewood, WI 99999
Phone: 444.555.6666   Email: john.mendoza@email.com

December 1, 2015

Mr. Joseph Wang
Partner
Sky High Executive Recruiting
1212 Elm Street
Milwaukee, WI 99999

Dear Mr. Wang:

I am contacting you in response to the posting on *The Ladders* for a CFO of Anchor Manufacturing Corporation in Chicago (posting #125-615). I am certain I would be an asset to Anchor's executive team.

My background and experience make me an excellent match for this position.
- 10+ years as Corporate Controller & Corporate Officer of a publicly-held global manufacturer and distributor
- Experienced in all financial aspects of M&A initiatives
- Proven track record in generating productivity gains and reducing expences in the finance organization
- Big "4" public accounting experience, including engagements in the U.S. and Mexico

In addition, I hold a CPA, received a BBA Magna Cum Laude and an MS in Accounting, and am fluent in English and Spanish. I am available to travel and/or relocate.

I look forward to discussing this opportunity further. My resume is attached. I can best be reached at 444.555.6666 or john.mendoza@email.com .

Sincerely,

John Mendoza

John Mendoza

Executive Headshot Suggestions

1. Headshots can be taken by a professional photographer or by a friend or family member with some facility using a camera. Regardless, the adage "a picture is worth a thousand words" applies a thousand-fold. People will make instant judgments about you when they view your headshot.

2. If the headshot is not done professionally, it is essential to "Photoshop" the background to a plain color. For most people, light grey works best; however, beige/tan or light blue may be better for others. There is a bright blue sometimes used for headshots that produces a less professional presentation. For someone familiar with Photoshop, it should only take a few minutes to remove your office, your living room, your backyard, or your front door from the photo.

3. Even professional photos sometimes err in the direction of an inappropriate pose, for example, the "hand under chin" that is commonly used in engagement pictures or a tilt of the head or body that looks more like it should be posted on a dating site. And, of course, this is not a Facebook photo from your last family vacation. Check out your contacts on LinkedIn and see which ones you think communicate well.

4. Attire in general: Wear what you would wear to an interview.

5. Attire for women: The focus should be on your face. Therefore, clothing should be tailored and not distract from the main attraction. Fashion forward is fine. Color is fine. Jewelry is fine. As long as it doesn't get in the way. Usually a jacket without a top underneath or a jacket with a silk tee photograph well. Collars on blouses rarely set right and can easily become dated as styles change. Whatever color, style, or jewelry you wear should complement your coloring and personal style. Pay attention to your hair and makeup so that it is effective for photography. You might consider having your hair and makeup professionally done.

6. Attire for men: The focus should be on your face. Standard business attire – suit and tie – is appropriate for most people most of the time. Select colors to complement your coloring and personal style. Err on the side of conservatism. Make sure that the collar on your shirt and your tie knot sit perfectly at your neck. If you don't know how to pick out the right clothes or you have difficulty with fit, get guidance at a good men's store. Get a good professional haircut. Make sure you have shaved recently – no 5 o'clock shadow.

7. Project the personal power, energy, and enthusiasm that engages the person looking at the photo. Have your headshot make the impression that you would want to make at an interview.

8. Relax and let the photographer do his/her job.

Note: For LinkedIn and certain other applications, your headshot is presented in a "square" format rather than a rectangle. For those, it is usually better to crop your photo to a square yourself and upload that rather than relying on the application to do it for you. You are less likely to get the top of your head chopped off.

Selected Corporate Assessments

Assessment	Cert or License Required*	Description
Myers-Briggs (MBTI) mbti.	Yes B	The MBTI® instrument continues to be one of the most trusted and widely used assessments in the world for understanding individual differences and uncovering new ways to work and interact with others. The **Form M** (Step I) assessment identifies a person's whole type made up of four basic type preferences. **Form Q** (Step II) provides a more richly textured picture of type and behavior using 20 additional facets. Form Q shows how each person expresses their type uniquely and individually.
Firo-B firob.	Yes* B	For more than 40 years the *Fundamental Interpersonal Relations Orientation-Behavior* (FIRO-B®) assessment has helped people around the world understand how their need for inclusion, control and affection can shape their interactions with others at work or in their personal life. Easy to administer and complete, the FIRO-B assessment is ideal for one-on-one coaching, team-building initiatives, communication workshops and leadership development programs. *MBTI® qualified practitioners are already qualified to use the FIRO-B assessment.*
• **Hogan Personality Inventory (HPI)** • **Hogan Development Survey (HDS)** • **Motives, Values, Preferences Inventory (MVPI)** • **Hogan Leadership Forecasts** • **Hogan Business Reasoning Inventory** HOGAN ASSESSMENT SYSTEMS	Yes B	The Hogan Assessment Suite consists of fourteen employee personality test and cognitive ability reports based on tests which have been scientifically designed for the workplace and rigorously validated with populations of working adults. All Hogan reports suggest a person's natural advantages, or "edges," and their potential problem areas, or "risks" in a job or business setting. They provide guidance and insight into hiring decisions, managing talent, and developing people for their next career moves. Hogan pioneered the use of personality tests for organizational decisions over 30 years ago. It is considered by many to be the gold standard in assessments for organizations today.
Lominger's VOICES 360° Feedback System LOMINGER International A KORN/FERRY COMPANY	Yes B	Lominger's VOICES® 360° instrument and system is perhaps one of the very best in the market. It can be easily customized using the 67 Leadership Architect Competencies. The companion book, ***FYI For Your Improvement***, by Michael Lombardo and Robert Eichinger, should be in the library of every corporate executive, manager, HR professional, and corporate coach. Now in its 4th edition, it's not cheap, but well worth the investment.

Assessment	Cert or License Required*	Description
The Birkman Method **BIRKMAN®** *Reaching Further*	Yes [B]	The Birkman Method® is a personality assessment that creates a multi-dimensional portrait of individuals highlighting their usual behaviors, stress behaviors, underlying needs and motivations and organizational orientations. It is used by coaches and corporations to facilitate team building, executive coaching, leadership development, career counseling, and interpersonal conflict resolution. It combines motivational, behavioral and interest evaluation into one single assessment, which provides a multi-dimensional and comprehensive analysis, thus reducing the need for multiple assessments.
Kolbe Indexes®	Yes [B]	The Kolbe Concept is based on understanding a person's "conative" instincts, which are separate and distinct from their feelings, intelligence, or personality traits (cognitive and affective). These creative instincts are manifested in an innate pattern that determines an individual's unique method of operation, or modus operandi (MO). A person's MO is quantifiable and observable yet functions at the subconscious level. It governs actions, reactions and interactions. When people act according to instinct, their energy is almost inexhaustible – like water running downhill. But when people are forced to act against their instinct, their energy is rapidly depleted – like water being pumped uphill. • The **Kolbe A** measures a person's instinctive method of operation (MO), and identifies the ways he or she will be most productive. • The **Kolbe B** Index measures an individual's expectations of how he or she should perform in a current job. Comparing a Kolbe B Index result with an A Index result yields insights into how to leverage instinctive talents at work. • The **Kolbe R** Index measures your expectations of another person in a relationship. Comparing one person's Kolbe R Index result with a partner's Kolbe A Index result provides insight into ways to improve the relationship. • The **Kolbe Y** Index measures the instinctive abilities of young people (4th–grade reading level to age 17). • The **Kolbe IF** for Kids is completed by parents or adult observers of children ages 2 to 8 and identifies the underlying pattern of a child's actions
Leadership Practices Inventory **LPI**	No [A]	The Leadership Practices Inventory® (LPI) is a 360 degree leadership assessment instrument created by bestselling authors James M. Kouzes and Barry Z. Posner (*The Leadership Challenge*) which has been used to assess the leadership behavior of nearly one million leaders worldwide. The instrument approaches leadership as a measurable, learnable, and teachable set of behaviors.

Assessment	Cert or License Required*	Description
DiSC	No [A]	The D.I.S.C. personality report or inventory, developed by William Moulton Marston, profiles four primary behavioral styles, each with a very distinct and predictable pattern of observable behavior. It's a nonjudgmental tool for understanding behavioral types and personality styles. Applied in corporate, business and personal situations, the DISC is used for personal growth and development, training, coaching and managing of individuals, groups, teams, and organizations. DISC is an acronym for: • **D**ominance - relating to control, power and assertiveness • **I**nfluence - relating to social situations and communication • **S**teadiness (submission in Marston's time)- relating to patience, persistence, and thoughtfulness • **C**onscientiousness (or caution, compliance in Marston's time) - relating to structure and organization
Emergenetics	Yes [B]	A popular and relatively new tool, Emergenetics is based on the latest brain research as well as extensive data from over 275,000 adults. This research indicates: 1) individuals have inborn traits to act and think in certain ways, and 2) these traits are modified and shaped as people interact with their surroundings. The combination of experiences and genetics intertwine to form some commonly recognizable patterns of personality traits. There are seven basic sets of attributes described by Emergenetics: four ways of thinking and three ways of behaving. • The four Thinking Attributes are Analytical preferences (Blue), Structural preferences (Green), Social preferences (Red) and Conceptual preferences (Yellow). • The three Behavioral Attributes (Purple) are Expressiveness behavior, Assertiveness behavior and Flexibility behavior.
Change Style Indicator	No [A]	The Change Style Indicator® is an assessment instrument designed to measure a person's preferred style in approaching change and dealing with situations involving change. The scores on this instrument fall on the change style continuum ranging from a Conserver style to an Originator style. A third style, the Pragmatist, occupies the middle range of the continuum. The three styles display distinct differences and preferences when approaching change.
Thomas-Kilmann Conflict Mode Instrument	No [B]	The Thomas-Kilmann Conflict Mode Instrument® (TKI) is the world's best-selling instrument for understanding how different conflict-handling modes, or styles, affect interpersonal and group dynamics and for learning how to select the most appropriate style for a given situation. The easy-to-use, self-scoring exercise is fast and powerful, and it can be done individually or in groups.

Assessment	Cert or License Required*	Description
Conflict Lens	Yes [B]	The Conflict Lens® is an assessment tool that is completed by individuals and then debriefed as part of a training session or training module on conflict resolution. It asks respondents to focus on one or two actual conflicts and to examine their thoughts, behaviors, and feelings in the process of managing the conflict(s). It also asks people to reflect on the outcomes of the conflict(s).
Campbell Interest & Skills Inventory	No [A]	The Campbell Interest and Skill Survey® (CISS) measures self-reported vocational interests and skills. Similar to traditional interest inventories, the CISS interest scales reflect an individual's attraction for specific occupational areas. It also adds parallel skill scales that provide estimates of an individual's confidence in his or her ability to perform various occupational activities. Together, the two types of scales provide more comprehensive, richer data than interest scores alone. The CISS focuses on careers that require post-secondary education and is most appropriate for use with individuals who are college bound or college educated.
Strong Interest Inventory	Yes [B]	The Strong Interest Inventory® assessments provide time-tested and research-validated insights to help your clients in their search for a rich, fulfilling career. Developed for career counselors and academic advisors who support college and high school students, as well as all practitioners who help adults with career decisions, the *Strong* empowers your clients to discover their true interests so they can better identify, understand, and often expand their career options.
StrengthsFinder Profile StrengthsFinder 2.0	No [A]	Derived from the book*, *Now Discover Your Strengths*, by Marcus Buckingham and Donald O. Clifton, this on-line instrument enables a person to complete a questionnaire developed by the Gallup Organization and instantly discover their own top-five inborn talents out of the 34 positive personality themes formulated by the authors. The access code for taking the instrument is provided in the book. A new and upgraded edition of the online instrument is now available—*StrengthsFinder 2.0*. *The book proposes that effective personnel management should be focused on enhancing employees' strengths rather than eliminating their weaknesses.*

Qualification or Certification Levels:

[A] **A Level Qualifications:** Assessments marked with the letter "A" and most books, guides, and programs are available for purchase without restriction.

[B] **B Level Qualifications:** To use these instruments, you must have either passed a licensed qualification program OR hold a bachelor's degree and have satisfactorily completed a course in the interpretation of psychological assessments and measurement at an accredited college or university.

Interview Preparation Worksheet

This Interview Preparation Worksheet provides a platform for personal preparation, positioning, and branding in advance of the potential stress of an interview. This method is quick and successful, giving you more confidence to deal with interviews fluidly and effectively.

Key Messages

List the important ideas from your profile statement that most effectively describe you and what you want to convey to interviewers. These "messages" should be stressed throughout the interview as you tell your story. If you are successful, the interviewer will remember you in terms of these messages. Target a maximum of 5 messages. Like a politician, you need to stay "on message."

Message (2-3 word phrase)	Detail Notes
Example: Startup Specialist	Started 2 high tech companies, bringing both to profitability within 24 months. One was acquired. One IPO'd.
1.	
2.	
3.	
4.	
5.	

Key Metrics of Performance

List facts that support your key messages. Having such facts at your finger tips translates to a more confident discussion once you understand how to incorporate each for impact. Remember you are positioning and branding your most important product, you.

Metrics may include revenue, profit (dollars or percentages), market share, product ranking, new customers, new vertical market entry, product development rollout, go-to-market successes, expense control, equity raised, stock price, collections, customer satisfaction, retention, unplanned turnover, and others. Supporting detail includes numbers that show performance on the metric.

Metric	Supporting Detail—Specific numbers and how you did it
Example: New Revenue	At ABC Company, grew revenue from $5 million to $20 million in 18 months, 50% above plan, by creating new product extensions.

Metric	Supporting Detail—Specific numbers and how you did it

Compensation Information

Compensation overview Describe your current compensation package in a 2-3 sentence overview from the detail below to position your compensation expectations concisely at a high level.	
Base	
Bonus and/or Commissions • Amount at Plan • Payment period • Last Paid • Guaranteed • Basis for Payment • Expectations for current period • Issues around pending payments	
Equity • Percent of company, if private • Total shares/options current value • Number of vested options, strike price • Number of unvested options, strike price, vesting date • Issues, pending payments	
Benefits	
Perks	

Relocation expectations • **Actual move** • **Temporary housing** • **Real estate assistance** • **Family relocation trips** • **Gross ups** • **Payment methods**	
Preferences • **Cash vs. Equity** • **Base vs. Incentives** • **Risk tolerance**	
List the top 3 – 5 factors related to compensation in your next job	

Position and Company Change History

Think through the reasons behind each and every change of position or company stated on your resume. Briefly describe the reason for leaving the old opportunity and joining the new. Reread your description of each change. What is the theme – positive, negative? If it's negative, rethink how you can position it to be positive or neutral at worst. In the overview section below, write a statement reflecting the theme that has resulted from your career moves, positioning to your advantage.

Career Overview Statement 2-3 sentences	
Company/Position *reverse chronological order—most current first like resume*	**Reasons**
	For leaving: For joining:
	For leaving: For joining:

Company/Position *reverse chronological order—most current first like resume*	Reasons
	For leaving: For joining:
	For leaving: For joining:
	For leaving: For joining:
	For leaving: For joining:

Strengths and Weaknesses

Strengths	How does this strength support your key messages?

Weaknesses	Restate this weakness to support your key messages.

Other Facts Important To How You Position Yourself

Fact	List	How does this support your key messages?
Three words you use to describe yourself		
Three words others use to describe you		
Long-term goals		
Mentors		
Industry participation		
Top five industry journals you read		
Top five most important books		
Activities or accomplishments outside of work		
Personal interests		

Post-Interview Self-Assessment Report

Company	
Position	
Interviewer, Title	
Contact Info	
Venue	__In-person __Telephone
Date and Length of Interview	
Strengths	
Areas for Improvement	
Ability to Engage the Interviewer	__High __ Medium __Low Comments:
Specific Recommendations	
Questions/Answers to Remember	
Follow Up Action Items	__Thank You __Documents? __Status? __Other?

ICF Core Competencies

A. Setting the Foundation

1. **Meeting Ethical Guidelines and Professional Standards** - Understanding of coaching ethics and standards and ability to apply them appropriately in all coaching situations
   a. Understands and exhibits in own behaviors the ICF Standards of Conduct (see list),
   b. Understands and follows all ICF Ethical Guidelines (see list),
   c. Clearly communicates the distinctions between coaching, consulting, psychotherapy and other support professions,
   d. Refers client to another support professional as needed, knowing when this is needed and the available resources.

2. **Establishing the Coaching Agreement** - Ability to understand what is required in the specific coaching interaction and to come to agreement with the prospective and new client about the coaching process and relationship
   a. Understands and effectively discusses with the client the guidelines and specific parameters of the coaching relationship (e.g., logistics, fees, scheduling, inclusion of others if appropriate),
   b. Reaches agreement about what is appropriate in the relationship and what is not, what is and is not being offered, and about the client's and coach's responsibilities,
   c. Determines whether there is an effective match between his/her coaching method and the needs of the prospective client.

B. Co-Creating the Relationship

3. **Establishing Trust and Intimacy with the Client** - Ability to create a safe, supportive environment that produces ongoing mutual respect and trust
   a. Shows genuine concern for the client's welfare and future,
   b. Continuously demonstrates personal integrity, honesty and sincerity,
   c. Establishes clear agreements and keeps promises,
   d. Demonstrates respect for client's perceptions, learning style, personal being,
   e. Provides ongoing support for and champions new behaviors and actions, including those involving risk taking and fear of failure,
   f. Asks permission to coach client in sensitive, new areas.

4. **Coaching Presence** - Ability to be fully conscious and create spontaneous relationship with the client, employing a style that is open, flexible and confident
   a. Is present and flexible during the coaching process, dancing in the moment,
   b. Accesses own intuition and trusts one's inner knowing - "goes with the gut",
   c. Is open to not knowing and takes risks,
   d. Sees many ways to work with the client, and chooses in the moment what is most effective,
   e. Uses humor effectively to create lightness and energy,
   f. Confidently shifts perspectives and experiments with new possibilities for own action,
   g. Demonstrates confidence in working with strong emotions, and can self-manage and not be overpowered or enmeshed by client's emotions.

C. Communicating Effectively

5. **Active Listening** - Ability to focus completely on what the client is saying and is not saying, to understand the meaning of what is said in the context of the client's desires, and to support client self-expression
   a. Attends to the client and the client's agenda, and not to the coach's agenda for the client,
   b. Hears the client's concerns, goals, values and beliefs about what is and is not possible,
   c. Distinguishes between the words, the tone of voice, and the body language,
   d. Summarizes, paraphrases, reiterates, mirrors back what client has said to ensure clarity and understanding,
   e. Encourages, accepts, explores and reinforces the client's expression of feelings, perceptions, concerns, beliefs, suggestions, etc.,
   f. Integrates and builds on client's ideas and suggestions
   g. "Bottom-lines" or understands the essence of the client's communication and helps the client get there rather than engaging in long descriptive stories,
   h. Allows the client to vent or "clear" the situation without judgment or attachment in order to move on to next steps.

6. **Powerful Questioning** - Ability to ask questions that reveal the information needed for maximum benefit to the coaching relationship and the client
   a. Asks questions that reflect active listening and an understanding of the client's perspective,
   b. Asks questions that evoke discovery, insight, commitment or action (e.g., those that challenge the client's assumptions),
   c. Asks open-ended questions that create greater clarity, possibility or new learning
   d. Asks questions that move the client towards what they desire, not questions that ask for the client to justify or look backwards.

7. **Direct Communication** - Ability to communicate effectively during coaching sessions, and to use language that has the greatest positive impact on the client
   a. Is clear, articulate and direct in sharing and providing feedback,
   b. Reframes and articulates to help the client understand from another perspective what he/she wants or is uncertain about,
   c. Clearly states coaching objectives, meeting agenda, purpose of techniques or exercises,
   d. Uses language appropriate and respectful to the client (e.g., non-sexist, non-racist, non-technical, non-jargon),
   e. Uses metaphor and analogy to help to illustrate a point or paint a verbal picture.

D. Facilitating Learning and Results

8. **Creating Awareness** - Ability to integrate and accurately evaluate multiple sources of information, and to make interpretations that help the client to gain awareness and thereby achieve agreed-upon results
   a. Goes beyond what is said in assessing client's concerns, not getting hooked by the client's description,
   b. Invokes inquiry for greater understanding, awareness and clarity,
   c. Identifies for the client his/her underlying concerns, typical and fixed ways of perceiving himself/herself and the world, differences between the facts and the interpretation, disparities between thoughts, feelings and action,

d. Helps clients to discover for themselves the new thoughts, beliefs, perceptions, emotions, moods, etc. that strengthen their ability to take action and achieve what is important to them,

e. Communicates broader perspectives to clients and inspires commitment to shift their viewpoints and find new possibilities for action,

f. Helps clients to see the different, interrelated factors that affect them and their behaviors (e.g., thoughts, emotions, body, background),

g. Expresses insights to clients in ways that are useful and meaningful for the client,

h. Identifies major strengths vs. major areas for learning and growth, and what is most important to address during coaching,

i. Asks client to distinguish between trivial and significant issues, situational vs. recurring behaviors when separating what is being stated and what is being done.

9. **Designing Actions** - Ability to create with the client opportunities for ongoing learning, during coaching and in work/life situations, and for taking new actions that will most effectively lead to agreed-upon coaching results

   a. Brainstorms and assists the client to define actions that will enable the client to demonstrate, practice and deepen new learning,

   b. Helps the client to focus on and systematically explore specific concerns and opportunities that are central to agreed-upon coaching goals,

   c. Engages the client to explore alternative ideas and solutions, to evaluate options, and to make related decisions,

   d. Promotes active experimentation and self-discovery, where the client applies what has been learned during sessions immediately afterwards in his/her work or life setting,

   e. Celebrates client successes and capabilities for future growth,

   f. Challenges client's assumptions and perspectives to provoke new ideas and find new possibilities for action,

   g. Advocates or brings forward points of view that are aligned with client goals and, without attachment, engages the client to consider them,

   h. Helps the client "Do It Now" during the coaching session, providing immediate support,

   i. Encourages stretches and challenges but also a comfortable pace of learning.

10. **Planning and Goal Setting -** Ability to develop and maintain an effective coaching plan with the client

    a. Consolidates collected information and establishes a coaching plan and development goals with the client that address concerns and major areas for learning and development,

    b. Creates a plan with results that are attainable, measurable, specific and have target dates,

    c. Makes plan adjustments as warranted by the coaching process and by changes in the situation,

    d. Helps the client identify and access different resources for learning (e.g., books, other professionals),

    e. Identifies and targets early successes that are important to the client.

11. **Managing Progress and Accountability** - Ability to hold attention on what is important for the client, and to leave responsibility with the client to take action
    a. Clearly requests of the client actions that will move the client toward their stated goals,
    b. Demonstrates follow through by asking the client about those actions that the client committed to during the previous session(s),
    c. Acknowledges the client for what they have done, not done, learned or become aware of since the previous coaching session(s),
    d. Effectively prepares, organizes and reviews with client information obtained during sessions,
    e. Keeps the client on track between sessions by holding attention on the coaching plan and outcomes, agreed-upon courses of action, and topics for future session(s),
    f. Focuses on the coaching plan but is also open to adjusting behaviors and actions based on the coaching process and shifts in direction during sessions,
    g. Is able to move back and forth between the big picture of where the client is heading, setting a context for what is being discussed and where the client wishes to go,
    h. Promotes client's self-discipline and holds the client accountable for what they say they are going to do, for the results of an intended action, or for a specific plan with related time frames,
    i. Develops the client's ability to make decisions, address key concerns, and develop himself/herself (to get feedback, to determine priorities and set the pace of learning, to reflect on and learn from experiences),
    j. Positively confronts the client with the fact that he/she did not take agreed-upon actions.

ICF Code of Ethics

Preamble

ICF is committed to maintaining and promoting excellence in coaching. Therefore, ICF expects all members and credentialed coaches (coaches, coach mentors, coaching supervisors, coach trainers or students), to adhere to the elements and principles of ethical conduct: to be competent and integrate ICF Core Competencies effectively in their work.

In line with the ICF core values and ICF definition of coaching, the Code of Ethics is designed to provide appropriate guidelines, accountability and enforceable standards of conduct for all ICF Members and ICF Credential-holders, who commit to abiding by the following ICF Code of Ethics.

Part One: Definitions

- **Coaching**: Coaching is partnering with clients in a thought-provoking and creative process that inspires them to maximize their personal and professional potential.

- **ICF Coach**: An ICF coach agrees to practice the ICF Core Competencies and pledges accountability to the ICF Code of Ethics.

- **Professional Coaching Relationship:** A professional coaching relationship exists when coaching includes an agreement (including contracts) that defines the responsibilities of each party.

- **Roles in the Coaching Relationship:** In order to clarify roles in the coaching relationship it is often necessary to distinguish between the client and the sponsor. In most cases, the client and sponsor are the same person and are therefore jointly referred to as the client. For purposes of identification, however, the ICF defines these roles as follows:

  - **Client:** The "Client/Coachee is the person(s) being coached.

  - **Sponsor:** The "sponsor" is the entity (including its representatives) paying for and/or arranging for coaching services to be provided. In all cases, coaching engagement agreements should clearly establish the rights, roles and responsibilities for both the client and sponsor if the client and sponsor are different people.

  - **Student:** The "student" is someone enrolled in a coach training program or working with a coaching supervisor or coach mentor in order to learn the coaching process or enhance and develop their coaching skills.

- **Conflict of Interest:** A situation in which a coach has a private or personal interest sufficient to appear to influence the objective of his or her official duties as a coach and a professional.

Part Two: The ICF Standards of Ethical Conduct

Section 1: Professional Conduct at Large

As a coach, I:
1. Conduct myself in accordance with the ICF Code of Ethics in all interactions, including coach training, coach mentoring and coach supervisory activities.

2. Commit to take the appropriate action with the coach, trainer, or coach mentor and/or will contact ICF to address any ethics violation or possible breach as soon as I become aware, whether it involves me or others.

3. Communicate and create awareness in others, including organizations, employees, sponsors, coaches and others, who might need to be informed of the responsibilities established by this Code.

4. Refrain from unlawful discrimination in occupational activities, including age, race, gender orientation, ethnicity, sexual orientation, religion, national origin or disability.

5. Make verbal and written statements that are true and accurate about what I offer as a coach, the coaching profession or ICF.

6. Accurately identify my coaching qualifications, expertise, experience, training, certifications and ICF Credentials.

7. Recognize and honor the efforts and contributions of others and only claim ownership of my own material. I understand that violating this standard may leave me subject to legal remedy by a third party.

8. Strive at all times to recognize my personal issues that may impair, conflict with or interfere with my coaching performance or my professional coaching relationships. I will promptly seek the relevant professional assistance and determine the action to be taken, including whether it is appropriate to suspend or terminate my coaching relationship(s) whenever the facts and circumstances necessitate.

9. Recognize that the Code of Ethics applies to my relationship with coaching clients, coachees, students, mentees and supervisees.

10. Conduct and report research with competence, honesty and within recognized scientific standards and applicable subject guidelines. My research will be carried out with the necessary consent and approval of those involved, and with an approach that will protect participants from any potential harm. All research efforts will be performed in a manner that complies with all the applicable laws of the country in which the research is conducted.

11. Maintain, store and dispose of any records, including electronic files and communications, created during my coaching engagements in a manner that promotes confidentiality, security and privacy and complies with any applicable laws and agreements.

12. Use ICF Member contact information (email addresses, telephone numbers, and so on) only in the manner and to the extent authorized by the ICF.

Section 2: Conflicts of Interest

As a coach, I:

13. Seek to be conscious of any conflict or potential conflict of interest, openly disclose any such conflict and offer to remove myself when a conflict arises.

14. Clarify roles for internal coaches, set boundaries and review with stakeholders conflicts of interest that may emerge between coaching and other role functions.

15. Disclose to my client and the sponsor(s) all anticipated compensation from third parties that I may receive for referrals of clients or pay to receive clients.

16. Honor an equitable coach/client relationship, regardless of the form of compensation.

Section 3: Professional Conduct with Clients

As a coach, I:

17. Ethically speak what I know to be true to clients, prospective clients or sponsors about the potential value of the coaching process or of me as a coach.

18. Carefully explain and strive to ensure that, prior to or at the initial meeting, my coaching client and sponsor(s) understand the nature of coaching, the nature and limits of confidentiality, financial arrangements, and any other terms of the coaching agreement.

19. Have a clear coaching service agreement with my clients and sponsor(s) before beginning the coaching relationship and honor this agreement. The agreement shall include the roles, responsibilities and rights of all parties involved.

20. Hold responsibility for being aware of and setting clear, appropriate and culturally sensitive boundaries that govern interactions, physical or otherwise, I may have with my clients or sponsor(s).

21. Avoid any sexual or romantic relationship with current clients or sponsor(s) or students, mentees or supervisees. Further, I will be alert to the possibility of any potential sexual intimacy among the parties including my support staff and/or assistants and will take the appropriate action to address the issue or cancel the engagement in order to provide a safe environment overall.

22. Respect the client's right to terminate the coaching relationship at any point during the process, subject to the provisions of the agreement. I shall remain alert to indications that there is a shift in the value received from the coaching relationship.

23. Encourage the client or sponsor to make a change if I believe the client or sponsor would be better served by another coach or by another resource and suggest my client seek the services of other professionals when deemed necessary or appropriate.

Section 4: Confidentiality/Privacy

As a coach, I:

24. Maintain the strictest levels of confidentiality with all client and sponsor information unless release is required by law.

25. Have a clear agreement about how coaching information will be exchanged among coach, client and sponsor.

26. Have a clear agreement when acting as a coach, coach mentor, coaching supervisor or trainer, with both client and sponsor, student, mentee, or supervisee about the conditions under which confidentiality may not be maintained (e.g., illegal activity, pursuant to valid court order or subpoena; imminent or likely risk of danger to self or to others; etc) and make sure both client and sponsor, student, mentee, or supervisee voluntarily and knowingly agree in writing to that limit of confidentiality. Where I reasonably believe that because one of the above circumstances is applicable, I may need to inform appropriate authorities.

27. Require all those who work with me in support of my clients to adhere to the ICF Code of Ethics, Number 26, Section 4, Confidentiality and Privacy Standards, and any other sections of the Code of Ethics that might be applicable.

Section 5: Continuing Development

As a coach, I:

28. Commit to the need for continued and ongoing development of my professional skills.

Part Three: The ICF Pledge of Ethics

As an ICF coach, I acknowledge and agree to honor my ethical and legal obligations to my coaching clients and sponsors, colleagues, and to the public at large. I pledge to comply with the ICF Code of Ethics and to practice these standards with those whom I coach, teach, mentor or supervise.

If I breach this Pledge of Ethics or any part of the ICF Code of Ethics, I agree that the ICF in its sole discretion may hold me accountable for so doing. I further agree that my accountability to the ICF for any breach may include sanctions, such as loss of my ICF Membership and/or my ICF Credentials.

For more information on the Ethical Conduct Review Process including links to file a complaint, you can go to the ICF website at www.coachfederation.org.

Adopted by the ICF Global Board of Directors June 2015

About the Authors

Mina Brown

Founder & President
Positive Coach LLC
positivecoach.com

Mina Brown is an experienced and masterful executive coach, career consultant, author, trainer, and public speaker. She provides individual and enterprise-wide executive coaching and industry accredited coach training. Before coaching, Mina was CFO of Aviall, Inc. and also SVP/GM of its Aerospace Division. Previously, she was in management with Ryder System and Amax. She started her career with Price Waterhouse. She is an ICF Professional Certified Coach (PCC), Board Certified Coach, Certified Hogan Coach, and Master NLP Practitioner. Mina holds an MBA from Vanderbilt University. A popular keynote speaker and workshop facilitator on a wide range of coaching topics, she is also a certified MBA/EMBA Coach for Vanderbilt's Owen Graduate School of Management.

Paula Asinof

Principal & Founder
Yellow Brick Path
yellowbrickpath.com

Paula Asinof is the founder of Yellow Brick Path, a career coaching, consulting, and resume services firm. She also advises Board of Directors candidates on their bios. Clients appreciate her straight talk, often unconventional perspectives, and the depth of her "real world" executive experience. Paula's background includes Executive Search recruiting and leadership positions in IT and Finance with GTE (now Verizon), Rand McNally, and the Chicago Stock Exchange. She began her career in public accounting. Paula holds an MBA from The Wharton School and an MA from Columbia University. She is a Credentialed Career Manager, Master Career Director, Certified NLP Coach, and an Associate of Career Thought Leaders.

Made in the USA
Las Vegas, NV
10 May 2023

71796140R00071